HOLY SPIRIT POWER

HOLY SPIRIT POWER

CHARLES SPURGEON

 *Whitaker House*

All Scripture quotations are from the *King James Version* (KJV) of the Bible.

HOLY SPIRIT POWER

ISBN: 0-88368-658-9
Printed in the United States of America
©1996 by Whitaker House

Whitaker House
30 Hunt Valley Circle
New Kensington, PA 15068

Library of Congress Cataloging-in-Publication Data

Spurgeon, C. H. (Charles Haddon), 1834–1892.
  Holy Spirit power / Charles H. Spurgeon.
      p.   cm.
  Originally published: New Kensington, PA : Whitaker
      House, ©1996.
  ISBN 0-88368-658-9 (pbk.)
      1. Holy Spirit.   I. Title.
BT121.3 .S68 2001
231'.3—dc21

                                          2001001395

    1 2 3 4 5 6 7 8 9 10 11 12 / 09 08 07 06 05 04 03 02 01

CONTENTS

ONE

THE COMFORTER

But the Comforter,
which is the Holy Ghost,
whom the Father will send in my name,
he shall teach you all things, and bring all
things to your remembrance,
whatsoever I have said unto you.
—John 14:26

That good old Simeon waited for *"the consolation of Israel"* (Luke 2:25), and so Jesus was. Before His actual appearance, His name was Day Star, which means "cheering the darkness" and is prophetic for the rising sun. The disciples looked to Him with the same hope that cheers the nightly watcher as he faithfully waits for the sun to rise in the morning. When Christ was on earth, He must have been the consolation of all those who were privileged to be His companions. We can imagine how readily the disciples ran to Christ to tell Him of their sorrows, and how sweetly, with that matchless intonation of His voice, He spoke to them and bade their fears be gone. Like children, they would consider Him as their Father.

Every want, every groan, every sorrow, every agony was promptly carried to Him; and He, like a wise physician, had a balm for every wound. He had a solution for their every care, and He readily dispensed mighty remedies for all of the fever of their troubles.

It must have been sweet to have lived with Christ. Sorrows were masked joys because they presented an opportunity to go to Jesus to have them removed. Oh, if only we could have placed our weary heads upon Jesus' chest and our births had been in that happy era when we might have heard His kind voice and seen His kind look as He said, *"Come unto me, all ye that labour and are heavy laden, and I will give you rest"* (Matthew 11:28).

When He was about to die, great prophecies and great purposes were to be fulfilled. Jesus had to go. He had to suffer so that He could be our redemption from sin. He had to slumber in the dust a while so that He might perfume the chamber of the grave.

His resurrection took place so that one day, we, the dead in Christ, might rise first and stand in glorious bodies upon earth. *"He ascended up on high"* so that He might make *"captivity captive"* (Psalm 68:18; Ephesians 4:8). He chained the fiends of hell, lashing them to His chariot wheels and dragging them high upon heaven's hill. This was to make them feel a second overthrow from His right arm when He dashed them from the pinnacles of heaven down to deeper depths beneath.

Hear how kindly Jesus spoke:

> *It is expedient for you that I go away: for if I go not away, the Comforter will not come unto you; but if I depart, I will send him unto you.* (John 16:7)

> *And I will pray the Father, and he shall give you another Comforter, that he may abide with you for ever.* (John 14:16)

He would not leave those few poor sheep alone in the wilderness. He would not desert His children and leave them fatherless. Before He left, He gave soothing words of comfort.

There are different meanings of the Greek word *paraclete,* which is translated here as *"Comforter."* Early translators employed transliteration, having left the original word in the Greek but transcribed it into our alphabet to form the word *paraclete*. As a name of the Holy Spirit, *Paraclete* has some other meanings besides "comforter." Frequently it means "monitor," "teacher," or "instructor." Often it means "advocate," but the most common meaning of the word is "comforter." Still, we can't pass over those other meanings without saying something about them.

THE HOLY SPIRIT AS TEACHER

Jesus Christ had been the official instructor of His saints while He was on earth. They called no man Rabbi except Christ. They sat not at the feet of men to learn their doctrines, but they heard them directly from the lips of Him who spoke as no other man has ever spoken. When Christ was to leave, where would people find another infallible teacher? Should they go to a Pope in Rome to be their infallible oracle? Should they lean on the councils of the church to decide all knotty points? Christ said no such things.

> *And I will pray the Father, and he shall give you another Comforter, that he may abide with you for ever.* (John 14:16)

Inserting the name of Instructor for Comforter, we can see Christ prayed for us to be sent another Instructor to be the person to explain Scripture, to be the authoritative Oracle of God, who will make all dark things light, who will unravel mysteries, who will untwist all knots of revelation, and who will make you understand what you could not discover had it not been for His influence. No man ever learns anything correctly unless he is taught by the Spirit. No man can know Jesus Christ unless he is taught by God.

There is no doctrine of the Bible that can be safely, thoroughly, or truly learned without the one authoritative Teacher. Tell me not of systems of divinity, of schemes of theology, of infallible commentators, of the most learned people, or of the most arrogant doctors, but tell me of the great Teacher who will instruct the sons of God and make us wise to understand all things.

The Holy Spirit is the Teacher. It matters not what this or that man says. I rest on no man's boasting authority, nor should you. You are not to be carried away by the craftiness of men or a sleight of words. The Holy Spirit is resting in the hearts of His children.

THE HOLY SPIRIT AS ADVOCATE

Another translation is "Advocate." Have you ever thought about how the Holy Spirit can be called an advocate? You know Jesus Christ is called Wonderful, Counselor, and mighty God, but how can the Holy Spirit be called Advocate? I suppose it is because He is our Advocate on earth to plead against the enemies of the Cross. How was it that Paul could so ably plead before Felix and Agrippa? How was it that the apostles stood without fear before the magistrates and confessed their Lord? How has it come to pass that God's ministers have been made as fearless as lions, their brows firmer than brass, their hearts sterner than steel, and their words like the language of God? It is simply that it was not the men who pleaded, but it was God the Holy Spirit pleading through them.

Besides this, the Holy Spirit is the Advocate in men's hearts. I have known of men who have rejected a doctrine until the Spirit began to illumine and enlighten them. We who are the advocates of the truth are often very poor pleaders. We spoil our cause by the words we use, but it is a mercy that the Holy Spirit will advocate successfully through us and overcome each sinner's opposition.

Did you ever know Him to fail, even once? Has God not convinced you of sin in the past? Did the Holy Spirit not prove to you that you were guilty even though no minister could ever get you out of your self-righteousness? Did He not advocate Christ's righteousness? Did He not tell you that your works were dirty rags? Did He not convince you of the judgment to come? He is the mighty Advocate when He pleads in the soul. He makes us aware *"of sin, and of righteousness, and of* [the] *judgment"* (John 16:8) to come.

Holy Spirit of Christ, Blessed Advocate, plead in my heart, plead in my soul, and plead with my conscience. When I sin, make my conscience bold to tell me. When I err, make my conscience speak at once; and when I turn aside to crooked ways, advocate the cause of righteousness and suggest I lie down in shame and confusion, knowing my guiltiness in the sight of God.

There is even another sense in which the Holy Spirit advocates. He intercedes for us as He advocates our cause to Jesus Christ *"with groanings which cannot be uttered"* (Romans 8:26). When my soul is ready to burst within me, my heart is swollen with grief, or the hot tide of my emotions is near overflowing from my veins, I long to speak, but the very desire chains my tongue. I wish to pray, but the fervency of my feeling curbs my language. There is a groaning within me that cannot be uttered.

Do you know who can utter that groaning, who can understand it, and who can put it into heavenly language and utter it in a celestial tongue so that Christ can hear it? It is God the Holy Spirit. He advocates our cause with Christ, and Christ then advocates it with the Father. He is the Advocate, and He makes intercession for us with groanings that cannot be uttered.

THE HOLY SPIRIT AS COMFORTER

Having explained the Spirit's office as Teacher and Advocate, I come now to the translation in our verse—the Comforter. Regarding this translation, I make three divisions: the Comforter, the Comfort, and the Comforted.

THE COMFORTER

First, God the Holy Spirit is our very *loving* Comforter. If I am in distress and want consolation, and if some passerby hears of my sorrow, steps in, sits down, and tries to cheer me; he speaks soothing words, but he loves me not. He is a stranger, who knows me not at all, and has only come to try his skill. What is the consequence? His words run over me like oil upon a slab of marble. They are like the pattering rain upon a rock; they do not break my grief, and I stand unmoved because he has no love for me.

On the contrary, let someone who loves me as dearly as his own life come and plead with me. Truly these words are music, and they taste like honey. He knows the password for the doors of my heart, and my ear is attentive to His every word. I catch the intonation of each syllable as it falls, for it is like the harmony of the harps of heaven. It is a voice in love, and it speaks a language that is its own. It is an idiom and an accent that none can mimic. Wisdom cannot imitate it, and oratory cannot attain it. It is love alone that can reach the mourning heart. Love is the only handkerchief that can wipe the mourner's tears away.

Is not the Holy Spirit our loving Comforter? Do you not know how much the Holy Spirit loves you? Can you not measure the love of the Spirit? Do you not know how great the affection of His soul is towards you? Go and measure heaven, weigh the mountains in scales, take the ocean's water and count each drop, and count the sand upon the sea's wide shore. When you have accomplished all of this, you can tell how much He loves you. He has greatly loved you, loved you for a long time, and will always love you. Surely He is the person to comfort you because He loves you. Admit Him into your heart so that He may comfort you in your distress.

Also, He is our *faithful* Comforter. Love sometimes proves unfaithful. Far more bitter than the gall of bitterness is to have a friend turn from me in my distress. Oh, woe of woes to have one who loves me in my prosperity forsake me in the dark day of my trouble. God's Spirit is not like this. He ever loves, and He loves to the end.

Trust Him. Maybe a little while ago you found the sweet, loving Comforter, and you obtained relief from Him. When others failed you, He sheltered you in His bosom and carried you in His arms. Oh, why distrust Him now? Away with your fears. He is your faithful Comforter.

You may say, "But I have sinned." So you have, but sin cannot sever you from His love; He still loves you. Do not think that the scars of your old sins have marred your beauty or that He loves you less because of that blemish. He loved you when He foreknew your sin, and He does not love you any less now. Come to Him in all boldness of faith, and tell Him that you are sorry that you grieved Him. He will forget your wandering and will receive you again. The kisses of His love will be bestowed on you, and the arms of His grace will embrace you. He is faithful, so trust Him. He will never deceive you. He will never leave you.

How *wise* a comforter is the Holy Spirit. Job had comforters, and I think he spoke the truth when he said, *"Miserable comforters are ye all"* (Job 16:2). Did people not comprehend his grief and sorrow? They thought that he was not really a child of God. They thought that he was self-righteous, and they gave him the wrong treatment. It is bad when a doctor mistakes a disease and gives a wrong prescription.

Sometimes when we go and visit people, we mistake their disease. We want to comfort them on a point where they do not require any comfort at all, and they would be better left alone than spoiled by such unwise comforters. But, how wise the Holy Spirit is. He takes the soul, lays it on the table, and dissects it in a moment. He finds out the root of the matter, sees where the complaint is, and either applies the knife where something is required to be taken away or puts a bandage where the sore is. He never makes mistakes. From every comforter except the Holy Spirit I turn, for He alone gives the wisest consolation.

Mark how *safe* a comforter the Holy Spirit is. All comfort is not safe. There is a very melancholy young man over there. He became so because he stepped into the house of God and heard a powerful preacher. The Word was blessed and convinced him of sin. When he went home, his father and the rest found that there was something different about him. "Oh," they said, "John is mad. He is crazy." His mother said, "Send him into the country for a week. Let him go dancing or to the theater."

Did John find any comfort there? No. They made him feel worse, for while he was there, he thought hell might open and swallow him up. Did he find any relief in the gaieties of the world? No, he thought they were an idle waste of time. They are miserable comfort, but they are the comfort of the world.

When a Christian is in distress, many may recommend this remedy or another. There have been many, such as infants, destroyed by the elixirs that were given to lull them to sleep. Many have been ruined by the cry of peace when there is none. They hear gentle things when they ought to be stirred to the quick. Cleopatra's serpent was sent in a basket of flowers, and men's ruin often lurks in fair and sweet speeches. Quite the opposite, the Holy Spirit's comfort is safe, and you may rest on it. Let Him speak the Word, and there is a reality about it. Let Him give the cup of consolation, and you may drink it to the bottom, for in its depths there is nothing to intoxicate or ruin. It is all safe.

Moreover, the Holy Spirit is our *active* Comforter. He does not comfort by words but by deeds. As in James 2:16, some people comfort by saying, *"'Depart in peace, be ye warmed and filled;'* [but] *notwithstanding* [they] *give them not those things which are needful to the body; what doth it profit?"* As this verse says, the words provide nothing. However, the Holy Spirit gives. He intercedes with Jesus, gives us promises, gives us grace, and in these ways, He comforts us.

He is always a *successful* Comforter. He never attempts what He cannot accomplish.

Remember, you never have to send for Him. Your Comforter is always *near* you, and when you need comfort in your distress, the Word is near you. It is in your mouth and in your heart (Romans 10:8). He is an ever-present help in times of trouble (Psalm 46:1).

THE COMFORT

Now, there are some people who make a great mistake about the influence of the Holy Spirit. A foolish man had a desire to preach in a certain pulpit. Even though he was quite incapable of the duty, he called upon the minister and assured him solemnly that the Holy Spirit revealed to him that he was to preach in his pulpit. "Very well," said the minister, "I suppose I must not doubt your assertion, but it has not yet been revealed to me that I am to let you preach. So, you must go your way until it is."

I have heard many fanatical people say that the Holy Spirit has revealed this original insight or that new idea to them. This is non-sense. The Holy Spirit does not reveal any-thing fresh now. He brings old things to mind.

> *But the Comforter, which is the Holy Ghost, whom the Father will send in my name, he shall teach you all things, and bring all things to your remembrance, whatsoever I have said unto you.*
> (John 14:26)

The canon of revelation is closed. There is no more to be added.

God does not give a new revelation, but He fixes and freshens the old one. When it has been forgotten and laid in the dusty chamber of our memory, He fetches it out and cleans the picture but does not paint a new one. There are no new doctrines, but the old ones are often revived.

It is not by any new revelation that the Spirit comforts. He does so by telling us old things over again. He brings a fresh lamp to manifest the treasures hidden in Scripture. He unlocks the strong chests where the truth had long been, and He points to secret chambers filled with untold riches. However, He mints no new coins, for enough is done.

There is enough in the Bible for you to live on forever. If your life should outnumber the years of Methuselah, there would be no need for a fresh revelation. If you should live until Christ comes back upon the earth, there would be no necessity for the addition of a single word. If you should go down as deep as Jonah or descend as David said he did into the belly of hell, there would be enough in the Bible to comfort you without a supplementary sentence. Christ said, *"All things that the Father hath are mine: therefore said I, that he shall take of mine, and shall show it unto you"* (John 16:15).

The Holy Spirit whispers to the heart. He says things such as, "Be of good cheer. There is One who died for you. Look to Calvary; behold His wounds; see the torrent gushing from His side—there is your Purchaser, and you are secure. He loves you with an everlasting love, and this chastisement is meant for your good. Each stroke is working your healing. By the blueness of the wound, your soul is made better." *"For whom the Lord loveth he chasteneth, and scourgeth every son whom he receiveth"* (Hebrews 12:6).

Do not doubt His grace because of your tribulation, but believe that He loves you as much in seasons of trouble as in times of happiness. And what is all your distress, when weighed in the scales of Jesus' agonies?

Especially at times when the Holy Spirit takes back the veil of heaven and lets the soul behold the glory of the upper world, then that saint can say,

> Oh, thou art a Comforter to me.
>> Let cares like a wild deluge come,
> And storms of sorrow fall.
>> May I but safely reach my home,
> My God, my heaven, my all.

Were I to tell of the manifestations of heaven, some of you could follow. You, too, have left sun, moon, and stars at your feet, while in your flight you outstripped the tardy lightning. You have seemed to enter the gates of pearl and to tread the golden streets while borne aloft on wings of the Spirit. But here, we must not trust ourselves because we could become lost in reverie and forget our theme.

THE COMFORTED

Who are the comforted people? I like to cry out at the end of my sermons, "Divide. Divide," because there are two parties. Some are the comforted, and others the comfortless. Some have received the consolation of the Holy Spirit, and others have not. Let me try to sift my readers to see which is the chaff and which is the wheat. May God grant some of the chaff to be transformed into His wheat.

You may say, "How am I to know whether I am a recipient of the comfort of the Holy Spirit?" You may know it by one rule: if you have received one blessing from God, you will receive all other His other blessings, too.

Let me explain myself. If I were an auctioneer and could sell the Gospel off in lots, I would dispose of it all. If I could say, "Here is justification through the blood of Christ, free, given away, *gratis*."

Many people would say, "I will have justification. Give it to me. I wish to be justified, and I wish to be pardoned."

Suppose I offered sanctification, the giving up of all sin, a thorough change of heart, leaving off drunkenness and swearing. Many would say, "I don't want that. I would like to go to heaven, but I do not want that holiness. I would like to be saved, but I would like to have my drink still. I would like to enter glory, but I must be able to curse on the road."

If you have one blessing, you will have all. God will never divide the Gospel. He will not give justification to one and sanctification to another, or pardon to one and holiness to another. No, it all goes together.

> *Whom he did predestinate, them he also called: and whom he called, them he also justified: and whom he justified, them he also glorified.* (Romans 8:30)

Oh, if I could lay down nothing but the comforts of the Gospel, you would swarm to them as flies do to honey! When you become ill, you send for the clergyman. You all want your minister to come then and give you consoling words. However, if he is an honest man, he will not give some of you a particle of consolation. He will not commence with pouring oil when the knife would be better.

I want to make a man feel his sins before I dare tell him anything about Christ. I want to probe into his soul and make him feel that he is lost before I tell him anything about the purchased blessing.

Have you been convicted of sin? Have you ever felt your guilt before God? Has your soul been humbled at Jesus' feet? And, have you been made to look to Calvary alone for your refuge? If not, you have no right to consolation. Do not take an atom of it. The Spirit comes to convict before He comforts, and you must have the other operations of the Holy Spirit before you can derive anything from this.

What do you know about the Comforter? Let this solemn question thrill through your soul. If you do not know the Comforter, I will tell you whom you will know. You will know the Judge. If you do not know the Comforter on earth, you will know the Condemner in the next world. He will cry, *"Depart from me, ye cursed, into everlasting fire, prepared for the devil and his angels"* (Matthew 25:41).

Well might Whitefield call out, "O earth, earth, earth, hear the Word of the Lord." If we were to live here forever, you might slight the Gospel. If you had a lease on life, you might despise the Comforter. However, you must die. Probably, some have gone to their long last home, and some will soon be among the glorified above or among the damned below. Which will it be for you? Let your soul answer. If you

fell down dead tonight, where would you be—
in heaven or in hell?

Do not be deceived. Let conscience have
its perfect work, and if, in the sight of God,
you are obliged to say, "I tremble and fear
that my lot should be with unbelievers," listen one moment. *"He that believeth and is
baptized shall be saved; but he that believeth
not shall be damned"* (Mark 16:16).

Weary sinner, the devil's castaway, repro-
bate one, wicked one, harlot, robber, thief,
adulterer, fornicator, drunkard, swearer,
Sabbath-breaker, I am addressing you as well
as the redeemed. I exempt no man. God has
said that there is no exemption here.

> *If thou shalt confess with thy mouth the
> Lord Jesus, and shalt believe in thine
> heart that God hath raised him from the
> dead, thou shalt be saved.*   (Romans 10:9)

Sin is no barrier, and your guilt is no ob-
stacle. Although as black as Satan or as deceptive as a fiend, whosoever believes will
have every sin forgiven, will have every crime
effaced, will have every iniquity blotted out,
will be saved in the Lord Jesus Christ, and
will stand in heaven safe and secure. This is
the glorious Gospel. May God make it hit
home in your heart and give you faith in Jesus.

We have listened to the preacher—
    Truth by him has now been shown;
But we want a Greater Teacher,
    From the everlasting throne:
Application is the work of God alone.

TWO

THE POWER OF THE HOLY SPIRIT

*Now the God of hope fill you
with all joy and peace in believing,
that ye may abound in hope,
through the power of the Holy Ghost.*
—Romans 15:13

All power is the special and peculiar prerogative of God and God alone. *"God hath spoken once; twice have I heard this; that power belongeth unto God"* (Psalm 62:11). God is God, and power belongs to Him alone.

He delegates a portion of His power to His creatures, yet it is still His. *"...The sun, which is as a bridegroom coming out of his chamber, and rejoiceth as a strong man to run a race"* (Psalm 19:4–5), has no power to perform its motions except as God directs. The stars, although they travel in their orbits and none could stop them, have neither might nor force except what God gives them. The tall archangel, near His throne, outshines a comet in its blaze, and though he is one of those who excels in strength and listens to the voice of the commands of God, he has no might except that which his Maker gives to him. As for Leviathan who makes the sea boil like a pot so that one would think the deep were white, or Behemoth who drinks up the Jordan in one gulp and boasts that he can snuff up rivers, and those majestic creatures that are found on earth, they owe their strength to Him who fashioned their bones of steel and made their tendons of brass.

Think of man. If he has might or power, it is so small and insignificant that we can scarcely call it such. Yes, even when it is at its greatest, when he sways his scepter, when he commands hosts, when he rules nations, the power still belongs to God.

This exclusive prerogative of God is to be found in each of the three persons of the glorious Trinity. The Father has power, for by His Word were the heavens made and all the host of them. By His strength, all things stand and fulfill their destiny through Him. The Son has power, for like His Father, He is the Creator of all things. *"All things were made by him;*

and without him was not any thing made that was made" (John 1:3). *"And he is before all things, and by him all things consist"* (Colossians 1:17). The Holy Spirit also has power. This is the power that I will discuss.

We will look at the power of the Holy Spirit in three ways: the outward and visible displays of it, the inward and spiritual manifestations of it, and the future and expected works of it. The power of the Spirit will then, I trust, be made clearly present to your souls.

The power of the Spirit has not been dormant. It has exerted itself. Much has been done by the Spirit of God already. More has been done than could have been accomplished by any being except the infinite, eternal, almighty Jehovah with whom the Holy Spirit is one person. There are four works that are the outward and manifest signs of the power of the Spirit: creation works, resurrection works, works of attestation or of witness, and works of grace.

THE WORKS OF CREATION

The Spirit has manifested the omnipotence of His power in creation works. Though not very frequently in Scripture, sometimes creation is ascribed to the Holy Spirit as well as to the Father and the Son. The creation of the heavens above us is said to be the work of

God's Spirit. This you will see at once by referring to Job 26:13: *"By his spirit he hath garnished the heavens; his hand hath formed the crooked serpent."* All of the stars of heaven are said to have been placed by the Spirit. One particular constellation called *"the crooked serpent"* is especially pointed out as His handiwork. He makes loose the bands of Orion, binds the sweet influences of the Pleiades, and guides Arcturus with his sons. He made all the stars that shine in heaven.

Also, those continued acts of creation that are still performed in the world, such as the bringing forth of man and animals with their births and generations, are ascribed to the Holy Spirit. If you look at Psalm 104, you will read,

> *Thou hidest thy face, they are troubled: thou takest away their breath, they die, and return to their dust. Thou sendest forth thy spirit, they are created: and thou renewest the face of the earth.*
> (Psalm 104:29–30)

The creation of every man is the work of the Spirit. The creation of all life and all flesh-existence in this work is as much to be ascribed to the power of the Spirit as the first garnishing of the heavens or the fashioning of the crooked serpent.

Look at the first chapter of Genesis, and you will see that peculiar operation of power upon the universe that was put forth by the Holy Spirit. You will then discover His special work. There we read,

> And the earth was without form, and void; and darkness was upon the face of the deep. And the Spirit of God moved upon the face of the waters. (Genesis 1:2)

There was one particular instance of creation in which the Holy Spirit was especially more involved. It was the formation of the body of our Lord Jesus Christ. Though our Lord Jesus Christ was born of a woman and made in the likeness of sinful flesh, the power that produced Him was entirely in God the Holy Spirit. As the Scriptures express it,

> The Holy Ghost shall come upon thee, and the power of the Highest shall overshadow thee: therefore also that holy thing which shall be born of thee shall be called the Son of God. (Luke 1:35)

He was begotten, as the Apostles' Creed says, of the Holy Spirit. The corporeal frame of the Lord Jesus Christ was a masterpiece of the Holy Spirit.

I suppose Christ's body excelled all others in beauty and was like that of the first man. I suppose it was the very pattern of what the body is to be in heaven when it will shine forth in all its glory. That fabric, in all its beauty and perfection, was modeled by the Spirit. In His Book were all the members written, *"when as of yet there was none of them"* (Psalm 139:13). The Holy Spirit fashioned and formed Christ, and here again, we have another instance of the creative energy of the Spirit.

THE WORKS OF RESURRECTION

A second manifestation of the Holy Spirit's power is to be found in the resurrection of the Lord Jesus Christ. If you have ever studied this subject, you have perhaps been rather perplexed to find that sometimes the resurrection of Christ is ascribed to Himself. By His own power and Godhead, He could not be held by the bonds of death, but since He willingly gave up His life, He had the power to take it again. In another portion of Scripture you find the power ascribed to God the Father: *"He raised him up from the dead"* (Acts 13:34). God the Father exalted Him. There are many similar passages. However, again, it is also said in Scripture that Jesus Christ was raised by the Holy Spirit.

Now, all these things are true. He was raised by the Father because the Father said for Him to be loosed. Justice was satisfied. God's law required no more satisfaction. God gave an official message that delivered Jesus from the grave. Christ was raised by His own majesty and power because He had a right to come out. He could no longer be held by the bonds of death. However, He was raised after three days by the Spirit and the energy that His mortal frame received. If you want proof of this, open your Bibles again and read the following:

> For Christ also hath once suffered for sins, the just for the unjust, that he might bring us to God, being put to death in the flesh, but quickened by the Spirit.
> (1 Peter 3:18)

> But if the Spirit of him that raised up Jesus from the dead dwell in you, he that raised up Christ from the dead shall also quicken your mortal bodies by his Spirit that dwelleth in you.   (Romans 8:11)

The resurrection of Christ, then, was effected by the agency of the Spirit. This is a noble illustration of His omnipotence.

Could you have stepped as angels into the grave of Jesus and seen His sleeping body, you would have found it to be as cold as any other corpse. If you had lifted up the hand, it would have fallen by the side. If you had looked at the eye, it would have been glazed. Moreover, there was a death-thrust that must have annihilated life. Even if you had looked at His hands, you would have seen that the blood did not distill from them. They were cold and motionless.

Could that body live? Could it rise up? Yes, and it is an illustration of the might of the Spirit. For when the power of the Spirit came on Him, as it was when it fell upon the dry bones of the valley, He arose in the majesty of His divinity. Bright and shining, He astonished the watchmen so that they fled away. He arose, no more to die but to live forever, King of Kings and Prince of the kings of the earth.

THE WORKS OF ATTESTATION

The third of the works of the Holy Spirit that have so wonderfully demonstrated His power are the attestation works. By these I mean the works of witnessing. When Jesus went for baptism in the river Jordan, the Holy Spirit descended upon Him like a dove and proclaimed Him God's beloved Son. This is what I call an attestation work. Afterward, when Jesus Christ raised the dead, healed lepers, spoke to diseases—which caused them to flee quickly—and propelled demons to rush in thousands from those who were possessed by them, it was all done by the power of the Spirit. The Spirit lived in Jesus without measure. All these miracles were worked by that power. These were attestation works.

After Jesus Christ was gone, the master attestation of the Spirit happened when He came like a rushing, mighty wind upon the assembled apostles. Split tongues of fire sat upon them, and He attested to their ministry by giving them the ability to speak with tongues as He gave them utterance. Also, miraculous deeds happened through them and how they taught. Look at how Peter raised Dorcas, how he breathed life into Eutycus, and how great deeds took place through the apostles as well as through their Master. Mighty signs and wonders were done by the Holy Spirit, and many believed because of them.

Who would doubt the power of the Holy Spirit after that? What will those Socinians—who deny not only the divinity of Christ, but also the existence of the Holy Spirit and His absolute personality—do when we get them on creation, resurrection, and attestation? They must rush from the very teeth of Scripture: *"And whosoever shall fall on this stone shall be broken: but on whomsoever it shall fall, it will grind him to powder"* (Matthew 21:44). The Holy Spirit has the omnipotent power of God.

THE WORKS OF GRACE

Other outward and visible signs of the power of the Spirit are works of grace. Picture a city where a soothsayer has power. Philip enters it and preaches the Word of God. Right away, Simon of Samaria loses his power and seeks for the power of the Spirit to be given to him. He fancies that it might be purchased with money. (See Acts 8:9–24.)

In modern times, picture a country where the inhabitants live in miserable huts and feed on reptiles and insects. Observe them bowing down before their idols and worshipping their false gods. They are so into superstition and so degraded and debased that you question whether they have souls or not.

Yet, look. Moffat goes with the Word of God in his hand and preaches as the Spirit gives him utterance to them. That Word is accompanied with power. The inhabitants cast aside their idols, and they hate and abhor their former lusts. They build houses in which to dwell. They also become clothed and are now in their right minds. They break the bow and cut the spear into parts. The uncivilized become civilized, and the savage becomes polite. He who knew nothing begins to read the Scriptures, and out of the mouths of Hottentots, God affirms the power of His mighty Spirit.

Picture a household in a city where the father is a drunkard, the most desperate of characters. There are many. See him in his madness. You might just as well meet an unchained tiger than meet such a man. He seems as though he could tear a man who offends him to pieces. Look at his wife. She, too, has a spirit in her, and when he treats her wrongly, she can resist him. Many brawls have been seen in that house, and often has the neighborhood been disturbed by the noise created there. As for the poor little children, see them in their rags and nakedness, poor untaught things. Untaught did I say? They are taught and well taught in the devil's school, and they are growing up to be the heirs of damnation.

However, someone whom God has blessed by His Spirit is guided to the house. He may be but a humble city missionary perhaps, but he speaks to people like them. "Oh," he says, "come and listen to the voice of God." Whether it is by God's own agency or a minister's preaching, the Word, which is quick and powerful, cuts into the sinner's heart.

The tears run down his cheeks as have never been seen before. He shakes and quivers. The strong man bows down. The mighty man trembles, and those knees that never shook begin to knock together. That heart, which never cowered before, now begins to shake before the power of the Spirit. He sits down on a humble bench as a penitent. He lets his knees bend while his lips utter a child's prayer. While it is a child's prayer, it is a prayer of a child of God. He becomes a changed character.

Mark the reformation in his house. That wife of his becomes the decent matron. Those children are the credit of the house. In due time, they grow up like olive branches around his table and adorn his house like polished stones. Pass by the house. There is no noise or brawl, but there are songs of Zion. See him, for there is no drunken revelry. He has drained his last cup, and now forswearing it, he comes to God and is His servant.

No longer will you hear at midnight the shout of revelry, but there should be a noise. It will be the sound of the solemn hymn of praise to God. Now then, is there not such a thing as the power of the Spirit? Yes, there is. We have all here witnessed it and seen it.

I know a village that was once, perhaps, the most profane in England. It was a village inundated by drunkenness and debauchery of the worst kind. It was nearly impossible for an honest traveler to stop in the local inn without being annoyed by blasphemy. It was a place known for radicals and robbers.

One man, the ringleader of all, listened to the voice of God. That man's heart was broken. The whole gang came to hear the Gospel preached, and they sat and seemed to revere the preacher as if he were a god and not a man. These men were changed and reformed. Everyone who knew the place affirmed that such a change could only be brought about by the power of the Holy Spirit.

Let the Gospel be preached and the Spirit poured out. You will see that it has such power to change the conscience, to improve the conduct, to raise the depraved, and to chastise and curb the wickedness of the race, that you must glory in it. There is nothing like the power of the Spirit. Only let it come, and indeed, everything can be accomplished.

THE INWARD POWER OF THE HOLY SPIRIT

Now then, the second point is the inward and spiritual power of the Holy Spirit. What you have already read may be seen, but what you are about to read must be felt. No man will apprehend what I say in truth unless he has felt it.

First, the Holy Spirit has a power over men's hearts, which can be very hard to affect. If you want to get them for any worldly object, you can do it. A cheating world can win a man's heart, and a little gold can win a man's heart. A trump of fame and a little clamor of applause can win a man's heart. Still, there is not a minister breathing who can win a man's heart by himself. He can win his ears and make them listen, and he can win his eyes and fix them upon him. He can win his attention, but the heart is very slippery.

The heart is a fish that all gospel fishermen have trouble holding. You may sometimes pull it almost all the way out of the water; however, slimy as an eel, it slips between your fingers, and you have not captured it after all. Many a man has fancied that he has caught the heart, but he has been disappointed. A strong hunter is needed to overtake the red deer on the mountains. It is too fast for a human foot to approach.

The Spirit alone has power over a man's heart. Do you ever try your power on a heart? If any man thinks that a minister can convert the soul by himself, I wish he would try. Let him go and be a Sunday school teacher. He will take his class, have the best books that can be obtained, have the best rules, draw his lines of protection about the house of his Spirit, and take the best boy in his class. If he is not tired in a week, I would be very much mistaken. Let him spend four or five Sundays trying, but he will say, "The young fellow is incorrigible."

Let him try another. And, he will have to try another and another and another before he will manage to convert one. He will soon find that it is as the Lord says in Zechariah 4:6: *"Not by might, nor by power, but by my spirit."* Man cannot reach the soul, but the Holy Spirit can.

"My beloved put in his hand by the hole of the door, and my bowels were moved for him" (Song of Solomon 5:4). He can give a sense of blood-bought pardon that will dissolve a heart of stone. He can

> Speak with that voice which wakes the dead,
> And bids the sinner rise:
> And makes the guilty conscience dread
> The death that never dies.

He can make Sinai's thunders audible. He can make the sweet whisperings of Calvary enter into the soul. He has power over the heart of man, and a glorious proof of the omnipotence of the Spirit is that He has rule over the heart.

However, if there is one thing more stubborn than the heart, it is the will. "My Lord Willbewill," as Bunyan calls him in *The Holy War*, is a fellow whose will cannot easily be bent. The will, especially in some men, is a very stubborn thing; in all men, if the will is once stirred up to opposition, there is nothing that can be done with them.

Somebody believes in free will. Many dream of free will. Free will. Where is that to be found? Once there was free will in the Garden of Eden, and a terrible mess free will made there. It spoiled all Paradise and turned Adam out of the garden. Free will was once in heaven, but it turned the glorious archangel out, and a third part of the stars of heaven fell into the abyss.

Yet, some boast of free will. I wonder whether those who believe in it have any more power over peoples' wills than I have. I know that I have none. I find the old proverb very true, "One man can bring a horse to water, but a hundred cannot make him drink." I do not think any man has power over his fellow creature's will; I know only the Spirit of God does.

"Thy people shall be willing in the day of thy power" (Psalm 110:3). He makes the unwilling sinner so willing that he is impetuous after the Gospel. He who was obstinate now hurries to the cross. He who laughed at Jesus now hangs on His mercy, and he who would not believe is now made by the Holy Spirit to do so willingly and eagerly. He is happy to do it and rejoices at the sound of Jesus' name. He delights to run in the way of God's commandments. The Holy Spirit has power over the will.

There is one more thing that I think is worse than the will. You may guess what I mean. The will is somewhat worse than the heart to bend, but there is one thing that excels the will in its naughtiness: the imagination. I hope that my will is managed by divine grace, but I am afraid that my imagination is not at times. Those who have a fair share of imagination know what a difficult thing it is to control. You cannot restrain it. It will break every rein. You will never be able to manage it.

The imagination will sometimes fly up to God with such a power that eagles' wings cannot match it. It sometimes has such might that it can almost see the King in His beauty and the land that is very far off. With regard to myself, my imagination will sometimes take me over the gates of iron, across that infinite unknown, to the very gates of pearl and discovery of the glorified.

It is just as potent in the other direction. My imagination has taken me down to the vilest kennels and sewers of the earth. It has given me thoughts so dreadful that while I could not avoid them, I was thoroughly horrified by them. These thoughts come, and the time when the plagues break out the worst is often when I feel in the holiest frame of mind, the most devoted to God, and the most earnest in prayer. However, I rejoice and think of one thing: I can cry out when this imagination comes upon me.

In Leviticus, when the maiden cried out against an evil act that was committed, her life was to be spared. So it is with the Christian. If he cries out, there is hope. Can you chain your imagination? No, but the power of the Holy Spirit can. He will do it, and He does do it at last. He does it even on the earth.

THE FUTURE AND DESIRED EFFECTS

Jesus Christ exclaimed, *"It is finished"* (John 19:30). This concerned Christ's own labor, but the Holy Spirit cannot say that. The Holy Spirit still has more to do, and until the consummation of all things, when the Son Himself becomes subject to the Father, *"It is finished"* will not be said by the Holy Spirit.

What, then, does the Holy Spirit have to do? First, He has to perfect us in holiness. There are two kinds of perfection that a Christian needs. One is the perfection by the justification of Jesus, and the other is the perfection of sanctification worked by the Holy Spirit. At present, corruption still rests in the heart of even the regenerate, the heart is partially impure, and there are still lusts and evil imaginations.

However, my soul rejoices to know that the day is coming when God will finish the work that He has begun. He will present my soul not only perfect in Christ, but also perfect in the Spirit, without spot, blemish, or any such thing (Ephesians 5:27). Is it true that my poor, depraved heart is to become as holy as that of God? Is it true that this poor spirit, which often cries, *"O wretched man that I am! who shall deliver me from the body of this death?"* (Romans 7:24), will get rid of sin and death? Is it true that I will have no evil things to vex my ears and no unholy thoughts to disturb my peace? Oh, happy day!

Oh, to be washed white, clean, pure, and perfect. Not an angel will be more pure than I will be, and not God Himself more holy. I will be able to say, in a double sense, "Great God, I am clean. Through Jesus' blood I am clean, and through the Spirit's work I am clean, too." Must we not extol the power of the Holy Spirit in making us fit to stand before our Father in heaven?

THE WORKS OF LATTER-DAY GLORY

Another great work of the Holy Spirit that is not yet accomplished is the bringing on of the latter-day glory. In a few more years, I know not when, and I know not how, the Holy Spirit will be poured out in a far different style from the present. *"There are diversities of operations"* (1 Corinthians 12:6), and during the last few years, the diversified operations have consisted in very little pouring out of the Spirit. Ministers have gone on in dull routine, continually preaching, preaching, preaching, and little good has been done.

The hour is coming when the Holy Spirit will be poured out again in such a wonderful manner that many will run back and forth, *"knowledge shall be increased"* (Daniel 12:4), and the knowledge of the Lord will cover the earth as the waters cover the surface of the great deep (Isaiah 11:9). When His kingdom will come and His will shall be done on earth as it is in heaven (Matthew 6:10), we are not going to be dragging on forever like Pharaoh with the wheels off of his chariot.

Perhaps there will be no miraculous gifts, for they will not be required. Yet, there will be such a miraculous amount of holiness, such an extraordinary fervor of prayer, such a real communion with God, so much vital religion, and such a spread of the doctrines of the Cross that everyone will see that the Spirit is truly poured out like water, and the rains are descending from above. Let us pray for this, continually labor for it, and seek it from God.

GREAT RESURRECTION POWER

One more work of the Spirit that will especially manifest His power is the general resurrection. From Scripture, we have reason to believe that while it will be triggered by the voice of God and of His Word (the Son), the resurrection of the dead will be brought about by the Spirit. The same power that raised Jesus Christ from the dead will *"also quicken your mortal bodies"* (Romans 8:11). The power of the resurrection is perhaps one of the finest proofs of the works of the Spirit.

My friends, if this earth could but have its mantle torn away for a little while, if the green sod could be cut from it, and we could look about six feet deep into its bowels, what a world it would seem. What would we see? Bones, carcasses, rottenness, worms, corruption. And you would say, "Can these dry bones live? Can they rise up?" Yes, *"In a moment, in the twinkling of an eye, at the last trump: for the trumpet shall sound, and the dead shall be raised incorruptible, and we shall be changed"* (1 Corinthians 15:52).

He speaks, and they are alive. See the bones scattered; they come together. See them naked; flesh comes upon them. See them still lifeless: *"Come from the four winds, O breath, and breathe upon these slain, that they may live"* (Ezekiel 37:9). When the wind of the Holy Spirit comes, they live, and they stand on their feet as an exceedingly great army.

PRACTICAL POWER OF THE HOLY SPIRIT

I have attempted to write about the power of the Spirit, and I trust that I have shown it to you. We must now have a moment or two for practical inference. Christian, the Spirit is very powerful. What do you infer from that fact? Infer that you never need to distrust the power of God to carry you to heaven. This sweet verse has been placed upon my soul:

> His tried almighty arm
>   Is raised for your defense;
> Where is the power can reach you there?
>   Or what can pluck you thence?

The power of the Holy Spirit is your bulwark, and all His omnipotence defends you. Can your enemies overcome omnipotence? They can then conquer you. Can they wrestle with Deity and hurl Him to the ground? They might then conquer you, for the power of the Spirit is our power, and the power of the Spirit is our might.

Once again, if this is the power of the Spirit, why should you doubt anything? Here are your son and your wife, brother, for whom you have pleaded in prayer so frequently. Do not doubt the Spirit's power. He may tarry, but wait for Him. There is your husband, holy woman, and you have wrestled for his soul. Although he is ever so hardened and quite a desperate wretch who treats you poorly, there is power in the Spirit. You, who have come from barren churches with scarcely a leaf upon the tree, do not doubt the power of the Spirit to raise you up. For it will be as a pasture for flocks, a den of wild asses (Isaiah 32:14), open but deserted until the Spirit is poured out from on high.

> *And the parched ground shall become a pool, and the thirsty land springs of water: in the habitation of dragons, where each lay, shall be grass with reeds and rushes.* (Isaiah 35:7)

You, who remember what your God has done for you personally, never distrust the power of the Spirit. You have seen the wilderness in glory like Carmel; you have seen the desert blossom like the rose. (See Isaiah 35:1–2.) Trust Him for the future. Then go out and labor with the conviction that the power of the Holy Spirit is able to do anything. Go to your Sunday school, your tract distribution, your missionary enterprise, and your preaching with the conviction that the power of the Spirit is our great help.

What is there to be said to you about this power of the Spirit? To me, there is hope for some of you. I cannot save you, and I cannot get at you. I may make you cry sometimes. However, you just wipe your eyes, and it is all over. Still, I know my Master can reach out and save you. That is my consolation. Chief of sinners, there is hope for you. This power can save you as well as anybody else. It is able to break your heart of iron and to make your eyes of stone run with tears. His power is able.

If He wills to change your heart, to turn the current of all your ideas, to make you at once a child of God, or to justify you in Christ, there is power enough in the Holy Spirit. He does not withhold from you, but you are restrained in your own affections and heart (2 Corinthians 6:12). He is able to bring sinners to Jesus.

He is able to make you willing in the day of His power. Are you willing? Has He gone so far as to make you desire His name, to make you wish for Jesus? Then, sinner, while He draws you, say, "Draw me, for I am wretched without you." Follow Him. Follow Him, and while He leads, tread in His footsteps.

Rejoice that He has begun a good work in you, for there is evidence that He will continue it even unto the end (Philippians 1:6). And, hopeless one, put your trust in the power of the Spirit. Rest on the blood of Jesus, for your soul is safe, not only now, but also throughout eternity. May God bless you.

THREE

THE HOLY SPIRIT, THE GREAT TEACHER

Howbeit when he,
the Spirit of truth, is come,
he will guide you into all truth:
for he shall not speak of himself;
but whatsoever he shall hear,
that shall he speak: and he will
show you things to come.
—John 16:13

To a great extent, this generation has gradually and almost imperceptibly become godless. One of the diseases of present-day mankind is the secret but deep-seated godlessness by which man has departed from the knowledge of God. Science has discovered second causes for us. Thus, many have forgotten the first Great Cause— the Author of all. They have been able to pry so far into these secrets that the great axiom of the existence of God has been too much neglected.

Even among professing Christians, while there is a great amount of religion, there is too little godliness. There is much external formalism but too little inward acknowledgment of God, too little living on God, living with God, and relying upon God.

The sad fact is that when you enter many of our places of worship you will certainly hear the name of God mentioned, but except in the benediction, you will scarcely know that there is a Trinity. In many places dedicated to the Lord, the name of Jesus is too often kept in the background. The Holy Spirit is almost entirely neglected, and very little is said concerning His sacred influence.

To a large degree, even religious men have become godless in this age. We sadly require more preaching regarding God—more preaching of those things that look not so much at the creature to be saved as at the Almighty to be extolled.

My firm conviction is that we will see a proportionately greater display of God's power and a more glorious manifestation of His might in our churches as we have more regard for the sacred Godhead, the wondrous Three in One. May God send us a Christ-exalting, Spirit-loving ministry. Men who will proclaim God the Holy Spirit in all His offices and extol God the Savior as the Author and Finisher of our faith. Men should not neglect that Great God, the Father of His people, who before all worlds elected us in Christ His Son, justified us through His righteousness, and will inevitably preserve us and gather us together in the consummation of all things at the last great day.

The subject of our text is God the Holy Spirit. May His sweet influence rest upon us. The disciples had been instructed by Christ concerning certain elementary doctrines, but Jesus did not teach His disciples more than what we might call the ABCs of religion. He gives His reasons for this in John 16:12, *"I have yet many things to say unto you, but ye cannot bear them now."*

Jesus' disciples were not possessors of the Spirit. They had the Spirit as far as the work of conversion was concerned, but they did not have it in the matters of bright illumination, profound instruction, prophecy, and inspiration. He said that He would send the Comforter and that when He had come, He would guide them into all truth. The same promise that He made to His apostles stands for all His children. In reviewing it, we will take it as *our* portion and heritage. We should not consider ourselves intruders on the property of the apostles or on their exclusive rights and prerogatives, for we conceive that Jesus says even to us, *"When he, the Spirit of truth, is come, he will guide you into all truth"* (John 16:13).

Concentrating upon our text, we see five things. First, an attainment is mentioned: a knowledge of all truth. Secondly, a difficulty is suggested: we need guidance into all truth. Thirdly, a person is provided: the Spirit will come and guide you into all truth. Fourthly, a manner is hinted at: He will guide you into all truth. Fifthly, a sign is given as to the working of the Spirit: we may know whether He works by His guiding of us into *"all truth"* (this is one thing—not *truths,* but *truth*).

ATTAINMENT OF TRUTH

An attainment is mentioned. This is a knowledge of all truth. We know that some conceive doctrinal knowledge to be of very little importance and of no practical use. I do not think so. I believe that the science of Christ crucified and the judgment of scriptural teachings are exceedingly valuable. I think it is right that the Christian ministry should not only be arousing but instructing. It should not merely be awakening but also enlightening, and it should appeal not only to the passions but to the understanding. I am far from thinking that doctrinal knowledge is of secondary importance. I believe it to be one of the first things needed in the Christian life —to know the truth and then to practice it. I scarcely need to tell you how desirable it is for us to be well taught in the things of the kingdom.

Nature itself, when it has been sanctified by grace, gives us a strong desire to know all truth. The natural man separates himself and interferes by meddling with all knowledge. God has put an instinct into man by which he is rendered unsatisfied if he cannot probe mystery to its bottom. He can never be content until he can reveal secrets. What we call curiosity is something that is given to us from God. It impels us to search into the knowledge of natural things.

That curiosity, which is sanctified by the Spirit, is also brought to bear in matters of heavenly science and celestial wisdom. David said, *"Bless the LORD, O my soul: and all that is within me, bless his holy name"* (Psalm 103:1). If there is a curiosity within us, it ought to be employed and developed in a search after truth. *"All that is within me,"* sanctified by the Spirit, should be developed. And truly, the Christian man feels an intense longing to bury his ignorance and to receive wisdom. If he desired terrestrial knowledge while in his natural state, how much more ardent is his wish to unravel, if possible, the sacred mysteries of God's Word? A true Christian is always intently reading and searching Scripture so that he may be able to certify himself as to its main and cardinal truths.

Not only is this attainment to be desired because nature teaches us so, but a knowledge of all truth is very essential for our comfort. I do believe that many persons have been distressed half of their lives from the fact that they did not have clear views of truth. For instance, many poor souls, under conviction, abide three or four times longer in sorrow of the mind than they would if they had someone to instruct them in the great matter of justification. There are believers who are often troubling themselves about falling away, but if they knew in their souls the great consolation that we are kept by the grace of God through faith unto salvation (1 Peter 1), they would no longer be troubled about it.

I have found some who are distressed about committing the unpardonable sin. However, when God instructs us, He shows us that no truly awakened conscience could ever commit that sin, because, when it is committed, the conscience is seared and causes no upset to the sinner. We would never fear or tremble afterwards, and all that distress would be alleviated. Depend on this, the more you know

of God's truth—all other things being equal—
the more comfortable you will be as a Christian. Nothing can give a greater light on your
path than a clear understanding of divine
things.

It is a mangled gospel, too commonly
preached, that causes the downcast faces of
Christians. Give me the congregation whose
faces are bright with joy, and let their eyes
glisten at the sound of the Gospel. I will then
believe that they are receiving God's own
words. Instead of joyful faces, you will often
see melancholy congregations whose faces
are not much different than the bitter coun-
tenances of poor creatures swallowing medi-
cine. This is because the Word spoken
terrifies them by its legality instead of comforting them by its grace.

We love a cheerful Gospel, and we think
that all the truth will tend to comfort the
Christian. Again, I hold also that this attainment of the knowledge of all truth is very desirable for the usefulness that it will give us
in the world at large. We should not be self-
ish. We should always consider whether a
thing will be beneficial to others. A knowledge
of all truth will make us very serviceable in
this world. We will be skillful physicians who
know how to take the poor distressed soul
aside, to put the finger on his eye, and to take
the scale off for him so that heaven's light

may comfort him. There will be no person, however perplexing his peculiar phase may be, to whom we will not be able to speak and to comfort.

He who holds the truth is usually the most useful of men. As a good Presbyterian brother said to me the other day, "I know God has blessed you exceedingly in the gathering of souls, but it is an extraordinary fact that nearly all the men I know, with scarcely an exception, who have been constructively employed in gathering in souls, have held the great doctrines of the grace of God." Almost every man whom God has blessed with the building up of the church into prosperity and every man around whom the people have rallied has been a man who has held firmly to free grace from first to last through the finished salvation of Christ.

A DIFFICULTY SUGGESTED

A difficulty is suggested. The difficulty is that truth is not so easy to discover. We need a guide to conduct us into all truth.

There is no man born in this world by nature who has the truth in his heart. There is no creature that was ever fashioned, since the Fall, who has an innate and natural knowledge of truth. Many philosophers have disputed whether there are such things as innate ideas at all, but it is of no use disputing whether there are any innate ideas of truth. There are none.

There are ideas of everything that is wrong and evil, but in our flesh, there dwells no good thing. We are born in sin and shaped in iniquity. Our mothers conceived us in sin. There is nothing good in us and no tendency toward righteousness. Then, since we are not born with the truth, we have the task of searching for it. If we are to be blessed by being eminently useful as Christians, we must be well instructed in matters of revelation. The difficulty is that we cannot follow the winding paths of truth without a guide. Why is this?

First, it is because of the very great intricacy of truth itself. Truth itself is no easy thing to discover. Those who fancy that they know everything and constantly dogmatize with the spirit of "We are the men, and wisdom will die with us," of course see no difficulties in the system they hold.

However, I believe that the most earnest student of Scripture will find things in the Bible that puzzle him. However earnestly he reads it, he will see some mysteries that are too deep for him to understand. He will cry out, "Truth, I cannot find you. I don't know where you are. You are beyond me, and I cannot fully view you."

Truth is a path so narrow that two can rarely walk together on it. We usually tread the narrow way in single file. Two men can seldom walk arm in arm in the truth. We believe the same truth in general, but we cannot walk together in the path, for it is too narrow.

The way of truth is very difficult. If you step an inch to the right, you are in a dangerous error, and if you swerve a little to the left, you are equally in the mire. On the one hand, there is a huge precipice, and on the other a deep swamp. Unless you keep to the true line, to the width of a hair, you will go astray. Truth is a narrow path indeed. It is a path the eagle's eye has not seen and a depth the diver has not visited.

Truth is like the veins of metal in a mine. It is often excessively thin and does not run in one continuous layer. Lose it once, and you may dig for miles and not discover it again.

The eye must perpetually watch the direction of the waterway of truth. Grains of truth are like the grains of gold in the rivers of Australia. They must be shaken by the hand of patience and washed in the stream of honesty, or the fine gold will be mingled with sand.

Truth is often mingled with error, and it is hard to distinguish it. However, it is said that we bless God, *"When he, the Spirit of*

truth, is come, he will guide you into all truth"
(John 16:13).

Another reason that we need a guide is
the harm caused by error. It easily steals
upon us, and if I may so describe our posi-
tion, we are often in a tremendous fog. We
can scarcely see an inch before us. We come
to a place where there are three turns. We
think we know the spot. There is the familiar
lamppost, and now we must take a sharp
turn to the left. On the contrary, we were
wrong. We ought to have gone a little to the
right.

We have been at the same place so often
that we think we know every flagstone.
There's our friend's shop over the way. It is
dark, but we think we must be quite right,
and all the while we are quite wrong and find
ourselves half-a-mile out of the way.

So it is with matters of truth. We think
that we are surely on the right path, and the
voice of the evil one whispers, "That is the
way, walk in it." You do so, and you find to
your great dismay that instead of the path of
truth, you have been walking in the path of
unrighteousness and erroneous doctrines.

The way of life is a labyrinth. The grassi-
est paths and the most bewitching are the
farthest away from the right. The most entic-
ing are those that are decorated with im-
proper truths.

I believe that there is not a counterfeit coin in the world that is as close to a genuine one as some errors are as close to the truth. One is base metal, and the other is true gold. Still, in externals, they differ very little.

We also need a guide because we are so prone to go astray. If the path of heaven were as straight as Bunyan pictured it, with no turning to the right or left, and no doubt it is, we are still prone to go astray. We could easily go to the right to the Mountains of Destruction or left to the dark Wood of Desolation.

In Psalm 119:176, David said, *"I have gone astray like a lost sheep."* That means very often, if a sheep is put into a field twenty times and does not get out twenty-one times, it will be because the sheep cannot. It will be because the place is boarded up, and the animal cannot find another hole in the hedge.

If grace did not guide a man, he would go astray, though there were signposts all the way to heaven. Even if it were boldly written, "This is the way to refuge," he would still turn aside. The avenger of blood would overtake him if some guide did not, like the angels in Sodom, put his hand on his shoulders and cry, *"Escape for thy life; look not behind thee, neither stay thou in all the plain; escape to the mountain, lest thou be consumed"* (Genesis 19:17). These, then, are the reasons why we need a guide.

A PERSON PROVIDED

A person is provided for us. This is none other than God, and this God is none other than a person. This person is *"he, the Spirit,"* the *"Spirit of truth,"* not an influence or an emanation but actually a person. *"When he, the Spirit of truth, is come, he will guide you into all truth"* (John 16:13). Now, we wish you to look at this guide to consider how adapted He is to us.

In the first place, He is infallible. He knows everything and cannot lead us astray. If I pin my sleeve to another man's coat, he may lead me part of the way rightly, but by and by, he will go wrong himself, and I will be led astray with him. But, if I give myself to the Holy Spirit and ask His guidance, there is no fear of my wandering.

Again, we rejoice in this Spirit because He is ever-present. We fall into a difficulty sometimes and say, "Oh, if I could take this to my minister, he would explain it. But, I live so far off, and I am not able to see him." That perplexes us, and we turn the text round and round and cannot make anything out of it.

We look at the commentators. We take down pious Thomas Scott, and, as usual, he says nothing about it if it is a dark passage. Then we go to holy Matthew Henry, and if it is an easy Scripture, he is sure to explain it.

But, if it is a hard text to understand, it is likely enough, of course, left in his own gloom. Even Dr. Gill himself, the most consistent of commentators, manifestly avoids the hard passages to some degree.

However, when we have no commentator or minister, we still have the Holy Spirit. Let me tell you a little secret: Whenever you cannot understand a text, open your Bible, bend your knee, and pray over that text. If it does not split into atoms and open itself, try again. If prayer does not explain it, it is one of the things God did not intend you to know, and you may be content to be ignorant of it.

Prayer is the key that opens the cabinets of mystery. Prayer and faith are sacred picklocks that can open secrets and obtain great treasures. There is no college for holy education like that of the blessed Spirit, for He is an ever-present tutor. We only have to bend the knee, and He is at our side, the great expositor of truth.

There is one thing about the suitability of this guide that is remarkable, and I do not know whether it has struck you—the Holy Spirit can guide us into a truth. Now, man can guide us *to* a truth, but it is only the Holy Spirit who can guide us *into* a truth. John 16:13 says, *"into."* Mark that word.

Now, for instance, it is a long while before you can lead some people to election, but when you have made them see its correct-ness, you have not led them *into* it. You may show them that it is plainly stated in Scrip-ture, but they will turn away and hate it. You take them to another great truth, but they have been brought up in a different fashion and cannot answer your arguments. They say, "The man is right, perhaps"—and they whisper, so low that conscience itself cannot hear—"but it is so contrary to my prejudices that I cannot receive it." After you have led them *to* the truth and they see it is true, how hard it is to lead them *into* it.

There are many who are brought *to* the truth of their depravity, but they are not brought *into* it and are thus not made to feel it. Some of you are brought to know the truth that God keeps us from day to day. However, you rarely get into it so as to live in continual dependence upon God the Holy Spirit and draw fresh supplies from Him. Get inside it.

A Christian should do with truth as a snail does with his shell: live inside it as well as carry it on his back and perpetually have it with him. The Holy Spirit, it is said, will lead us into all truth. You may be brought to a chamber where there is an abundance of gold and silver, but you will be no richer unless you achieve an entrance. It is the Spirit's work to unbar the two-leafed gates and to bring us into the truth so that we may get inside it. As dear old Rowland Hill said, "Not only hold the truth, but have the truth hold us."

A METHOD SUGGESTED

A method is suggested: *"He will guide you into all truth"* (John 16:13). Now, I must give an illustration. I want to compare truth to some cave or grotto of which you have heard. Its wondrous stalactites hang from the roof, and echoing stalagmites start from the floor. It is a cavern that glitters with lustrous minerals and abounds in marvels. Before entering the cavern, you inquire for a guide. He comes with his flaming torch and leads you down to a considerable depth. You find yourself in the midst of the cave, and he leads you through different chambers. Here, he points to a little stream rushing from amid the rocks, indicating its rise and progress. There, he points to some peculiar rock and tells you its name. Then, he takes you into a large natural hall and tells you how many persons once feasted in it, and so on.

Truth is a grand series of caverns, and it is our glory to have so great and wise a Conductor and Guide. Imagine that we are coming into the darkness of the innermost cavern. He is a light shining in the midst of us to guide us. And, by the light, He shows us wondrous things.

The Holy Spirit teaches us in three ways: suggestion, direction, and illumination. First, He guides us into all truth by *suggestion.* There are thoughts dwelling in our minds, which were not born there, but were imported from heaven and put there by the Spirit. We do not vainly imagine that angels whisper in our ears and that devils do the same.

Both good and evil spirits hold conversations with men, and some of us have experienced this. We have had strange thoughts, which were not the offspring of our souls but which came from angelic visitors. Direct temptations and evil insinuations have also been had, which were not brewed in our own souls but which came from the pestilential cauldron of hell. So, the Spirit speaks in men's ears. Sometimes He speaks in the darkness of the night. In ages gone by, He spoke in dreams and visions, but now He speaks by His Word.

Have you not at times had a thought, concerning God and heavenly things, in the middle of your business and you could not tell where it came from? Have you not been reading or studying the Scripture when a text came to your mind? You could not help it, but even though you put it down, it was like cork in water and would swim up again to the top of your mind. Well, that good thought was put there by the Spirit. He often guides His people into all truth by *suggesting,* just as the guide in the grotto does with his torch. The cavern guide does not say a word, perhaps, but he walks into a passage himself, and you follow him. So, the Spirit suggests a thought, and your heart follows it up.

I well recall the manner in which I learned the doctrines of grace in a single instant. Born, as all of us are by nature, an Arminian, I still believed the old things that I had heard continually from the pulpit, and I did not see the grace of God. I remember sitting in the house of God one day and hearing a sermon that was as dry as possible and as worthless as all such sermons are. A thought struck my mind, *How did I come to be converted?* I prayed. I then wondered, *How did I come to pray?* I was induced to pray by reading the Scriptures. *How did I come to read the Scriptures?* And then, in a moment, I saw that God was at the bottom of it all and that He is the Author of faith. It was then that the whole doctrine opened up to me from which I have not departed.

Sometimes, however, He leads us by *direction.* The guide points and says, "There, go along that particular path. That is the way." In the same way, the Spirit gives direction and tendency to our thoughts. He is not suggesting a new one, but He is letting a particular thought, once started, take such and such a direction. He is not so much putting a boat on the stream as He is steering it when it is there. When our thoughts are considering sacred things, He leads us into a more excellent channel from that in which we started.

Time after time, you have started a meditation on a certain doctrine and have unaccountably been gradually led away into another. You saw how one doctrine leaned on another, as is the case with the stones in the arch of a bridge, all hanging on the keystone of Jesus Christ crucified. You were brought to see these things not by a new suggested idea but by direction given to your thoughts.

Perhaps the best way in which the Holy Spirit leads us into all truth is by *illumination*. He illuminates the Bible. Now, do any of you have an illuminated Bible?

"No," says one, "I have a leather Bible."

Another says, "I have a marginal reference Bible."

That is all very well, but do you have an illuminated Bible?

"Yes," says yet another, "I have a large family Bible with pictures in it. There is a picture of John the Baptist baptizing Christ by pouring water on His head."

There are many other nonsensical things as well, but that is not what I mean by an illuminated Bible. "I have a Bible with splendid engravings in it," says another. I know you may have, but do you have an illuminated Bible?

Finally, someone says, "I do not understand what you mean by an illuminated Bible." Well, it is the Christian man who has an illuminated Bible. He does not buy it illuminated originally, but when he reads it,

> A glory gilds the sacred page,
>   Majestic like the sun;
> Which gives a light to every age,
>   It gives, but borrows none.

There is nothing like reading an illuminated Bible. You may read for all eternity and never learn anything from it unless it is illuminated by the Spirit. Then, the words shine forth like stars. The book seems as if it is made of gold leaf. Every single letter glitters like a diamond. Oh, it is a blessed thing to read an illuminated Bible lit up by the radiance of the Holy Spirit!

Have you read the Bible and studied it only to find that your eyes are still unenlightened? Go and say, "Oh, Lord, gild the Bible for me. I want an expounded Bible. Illuminate it, and shine upon it, for I cannot read it profitably unless you enlighten me."

Blind men may read the Bible with their fingers, but blind souls cannot. We want a light to read the Bible by, for there is no reading it in the dark. Thus, the Holy Spirit leads us into all truth by suggesting ideas, directing our thoughts, and illuminating the Scriptures when we read them.

AN EVIDENCE

The question may be arising in you, "How may I know whether I am enlightened by the influence of the Holy Spirit and led into all truth?" First, you may know the Holy Spirit's influence by His *unity*. He guides us into all *truth*. Secondly, you may know the Spirit's influence by its *universality*. He guides us into *all* truth.

Regarding unity, if you are judging a minister as to whether he has the Holy Spirit in him or not, you may know him in the first place by the constant unity of his testimony. A man cannot be enlightened by the Holy Spirit if he sometimes says yes and sometimes says no. The Spirit never says one thing at one time and another thing at another time. Indeed, there are many good men who say both yes and no, but their contrary testimonies are not both from God the Spirit. God the Spirit cannot witness to black and white, to a falsehood and a truth.

It has always been held as a first principle that truth is *one* thing. Some persons say, "I find one thing in one part of the Bible and another thing in another part, and though it contradicts itself, I must believe it." All quite right, brother, if it did contradict itself, but the fault is not in the wood but in the carpenter. Just as many carpenters do not understand dovetailing, so it is that many preachers do not understand dovetailing. It is very nice work, and it is not easily learned. It takes some apprenticeship to make all doctrines fit neatly together.

You may also know if you are led by the Spirit's influence and guided into all truth by its universality. The true child of God will not be led into some truth, but into all truth. When he first starts, he will not know half of the truth. He will believe it but will not understand it. He will have a small bit of it but not the sum total in all its breadth and length.

There is nothing like learning through experience. A man cannot become a theologian in a week. Certain doctrines take years to develop themselves. Like aloe that takes a hundred years to be readied, there are some truths that must long lie in the heart before they really come out and make themselves appear, so that we can speak of them as what we do know and testify of that which we have seen.

The Spirit will gradually lead us into all truth. For instance, if it is true that Jesus

Christ is to reign upon the earth personally for a thousand years, as I am inclined to believe it is, if I am under the Spirit, that will be more and more revealed to me until I declare it with confidence. Some men begin very timidly. At first, a man says, "I know we are justified by faith, and I have peace with God, but so many have cried out against eternal justification that I am afraid of it." However, he is gradually enlightened and led to see that in the same hour when all his debts were paid, a full discharge was given. He sees that in the moment when sin was canceled, every elect soul was justified in God's mind even though they were not justified in their own minds until afterward. The Spirit will lead you into all truth.

Now, what are the practical inferences from this great doctrine? The first is with reference to the Christian who is afraid of his own ignorance. There are many who are just enlightened and have tasted of heavenly things, but they are afraid that they are too ignorant to be saved. The Holy Spirit can teach anyone, regardless of how illiterate or uninstructed he might be.

I have known some men who were almost idiots before conversion, but they afterwards had their faculties wonderfully developed. Some time ago, there was a man who was so ignorant that he could not read, and never in his life did he speak anything with proper grammar unless it was by mistake. Moreover, he was considered to be what the people in his neighborhood called "daft." But, when he was converted, the first thing he did was pray. He stammered out a few words, and in little time, his powers of speaking began to develop themselves. Then, he thought he would like to read the Scriptures. After long, long months of labor, he learned to read. What was the next thing? He thought he could preach, and he did preach a little in his own homely way in his house. He thought, "I must read a few more books." His mind expanded, and he became a useful minister, settled in a country village, laboring for God.

Little intellect is needed to be taught of God. If you feel your ignorance, do not despair. Go to the Spirit, the great Teacher, and ask His sacred influence. It will come to pass that He *"will guide you into all truth"* (John 16:13).

Whenever any of our fellow Christians do not understand the truth, let us take a hint as to the best way of dealing with them. Do not dispute with them. I have heard many controversies, but I have never heard of any good coming from one of them. Few men are taught by controversy. The axiom rings true: "A man convinced against his will is of the same opinion still." Pray for them that the

Spirit of truth may lead them *"into all truth."* Do not be angry with your brother, but pray for him. Cry, "Lord, open his eyes that he may behold wondrous things from your law."

Lastly, some of you know nothing about the Spirit of truth or about the truth itself. It may be that some of you are saying, "We care little about which of you is right. We are happily indifferent to it." Poor sinner, if you knew the gift of God and who it was that spoke the truth, you would not say, "I don't care about it." If you only knew how essential the truth is to your salvation, you would not talk in such a way. The truth of God is that you are a worthless sinner who must believe that God, from all eternity, apart from all of your merits, loved you and bought you with the Redeemer's blood. He justified you in the forum of heaven and will justify you by and by in the forum of your conscience through the Holy Spirit by faith. If you knew that there is a heaven for you beyond the chance of a failure and a crown for you, the luster of which can never be dimmed, then you would say, "Indeed the truth is precious to my soul."

Why, these men of error want to take away the truth, which alone can save you, the only gospel that can deliver you from hell. They deny the great truths of free grace—those fundamental doctrines that alone can snatch a sinner from hell. Even though you do not feel interested in them now, I still would say that you ought to desire to see them promoted. May God have you know the truth in your hearts. May the Spirit *"guide you into all truth"* (John 16:13). For if you do not know the truth here, learning of it will be sorrowful in the dark chambers of the pit where the only light shall be the flames of hell. May you know the truth here.

"The truth shall make you free" (John 8:32), and *"If the Son therefore shall make you free, ye shall be free indeed"* (John 8:36), for He says, *"I am the way, the truth, and the life"* (John 14:6). Believe on Jesus, you chief of sinners. Trust His love and mercy, and you will be saved, for God the Spirit gives faith and eternal life.

FOUR

THE WITHERING WORK OF THE SPIRIT

*The voice said, Cry. And he said, What
shall I cry? All flesh is grass, and all
the goodliness thereof is as the flower of the
field: The grass withereth, the flower fadeth:
because the spirit of the LORD bloweth upon it:
surely the people is grass.
The grass withereth, the flower fadeth:
but the word of our God shall stand for ever.*
—Isaiah 40:6–8

*Being born again, not of corruptible seed,
but of incorruptible, by the word of God,
which liveth and abideth for ever.
For all flesh is as grass, and all the glory
of man as the flower of grass.
The grass withereth, and the flower
thereof falleth away:
But the word of the Lord endureth for ever.
And this is the word which by the gospel is
preached unto you.*
—1 Peter 1:23–25

This passage from Isaiah may be used as a very eloquent description of our mortality. If a sermon was preached from it upon the frailty of human nature, the brevity of life, and the certainty of death, no one could dispute the appropriateness of the text. Yet, I venture to question whether such a discourse would strike the central teaching of the prophet.

Something more than the decay of our material flesh is intended here. The carnal mind, the flesh in another sense, was intended by the Holy Spirit when He had His messenger proclaim those words. By the context, it does not seem to me that a mere expression of the mortality of our race was needed. It would hardly keep pace with the sublime revelations that surround it, and it would, in some measure, be a digression from the subject at hand.

The notion that we are simply reminded of here, our mortality, does not square with the New Testament exposition of it in Peter, which I have also placed before you as a text. There is another, more spiritual meaning here beyond that which would be contained in the great and very obvious truth: all of us must die.

Look at the chapter in Isaiah with care. What is the subject of it? It is the divine consolation of Zion. Zion had been tossed back and forth with conflicts. She had been smarting with the sting of sin. The Lord, to remove her sorrow, had His prophets announce the coming of the long-expected Deliverer, the end and accomplishment of all her warfare, and the pardon of her iniquity. There is no doubt that this is the theme of the prophecy, and there is no sort of question about the next point.

This point is that Isaiah goes on to foretell the coming of John the Baptist as the forerunner of the Messiah. We have no difficulty in the explanation of the passage,

> The voice of him that crieth in the wilderness, Prepare ye the way of the LORD, make straight in the desert a highway for our God. (Isaiah 40:3)

The New Testament refers this again and again to John the Baptist and his ministry. The object of the coming of the Baptist and the mission of the Messiah, whom he spoke of, was the manifestation of divine glory.

Observe Isaiah 40:5, *"And the glory of the LORD shall be revealed, and all flesh shall see it together: for the mouth of the LORD hath spoken it."* Well, what next? Was it necessary to mention man's mortality in this connection? I think not. However, there is much more in the way of appropriateness to the succeeding verses if we see their deeper meaning. Do they not mean this?

In order to make room for the display of the divine glory in Christ Jesus and His salvation, there would come a withering of all the glory man boasts of himself. The flesh should be seen for its truly corrupt and dying nature so that the grace of God alone may be exalted. This would be seen under the ministry of John the Baptist first and should be the preparatory work of the Holy Spirit in men's hearts, in all time, so that the glory of the Lord will be revealed and human pride will be forever confounded.

The Spirit blows upon the flesh, and what seems vigorous becomes weak. What was fair to look upon is smitten with decay, and the true nature of the flesh is discovered. Its deceit is laid bare, and its power is destroyed. There is space for the dispensation of the ever-abiding Word and for the rule of the Great Shepherd, whose words are spirit and life (John 6:36).

There is also a withering brought by the Spirit that is the preparation for the sowing and implanting by which salvation is brought about. The withering before the sowing was marvelously fulfilled in the preaching of John the Baptist. Appropriately, he carried on his ministry in the desert, for a spiritual desert was all around him. His was *the voice of one crying in the wilderness"* (Matthew 3:3). It was not his work to plant. His job was to cut down.

The fleshly religion of the Jews was then in its prime. Pharisaism stalked the streets in all its pomp. Men complacently rested in outward ceremonies only, and spiritual relig- ion was at the lowest conceivable ebb. Here and there a Simeon and an Anna may have been found, but for the most part, men knew nothing of spiritual religion. They said in their hearts, *"'We have Abraham to our fa- ther,'* and this is enough" (Matthew 3:9). What a stir he made when he called the lordly Pharisees a generation of vipers and said, *"Repent ye: for the kingdom of heaven is at hand"* (Matthew 3:2). How he shook the na- tion with the declaration, *"Now also the ax is laid unto the root of the trees"* (Matthew 3:10). Stern as Elijah, his work was to level the mountains and to lay low every lofty imagi- nation.

The word *repent* was as a scorching wind to the foliage of self-righteousness. It was a killing blast for the confidence of ceremonial- ism. His food and his dress called for fasting and mourning. The outward token of his ministry declared the death amid which he preached, as he buried in the waters of the Jordan those who came to him. This was the meaning of the emblem that he set before the crowd. His typical act was as thorough in its teaching as were his words. Plus, he warned them of a yet more searching and trying baptism with the Holy Spirit and with fire, and of the coming of One *"whose fan is in His hand, and He will thoroughly purge His floor"* (Matthew 3:12). The Spirit in John the Baptist blew as the rough north wind, searching and withering, and it made him a destroyer of the vanities of a fleshly religion. This was done so that the spiritual faith might be established.

When our Lord Himself appeared, He came into a withered land whose glories had all departed. Old Jesse's stem was bare, and our Lord was the branch that grew out of his root. The scepter had departed from Judah, and the lawgiver from between his feet, when Shiloh came (Genesis 9:10). An alien sat on David's throne, and the Romans called the covenant land their own. The lamp of prophecy burned dimly, if it had not utterly gone out. No Isaiah had come forth at that time to console them, not even a Jeremiah to lament the abandonment of their faith.

The whole economy of Judaism was as worn-out clothes. It had waxed old, and it was ready to vanish away. The priesthood was in disarray. Luke tells us that Annas and Caiaphas were high priests that year—two in a year or at once—a strange setting aside of the laws of Moses. All the dispensation that gathered around the visible, or as Paul called it, *"a worldly sanctuary"* (Hebrews 9:1), was coming to a close.

When our Lord had finished His work, the veil of the temple was torn in two, the sacrifices were abolished, the priesthood of Aaron was set aside, and carnal ordinances were abrogated, for the Spirit revealed spiritual things. When He came who was made a priest, *"not after the law of a carnal commandment, but after the power of an endless life"* (Hebrews 7:16), there was *"a disannulling of the commandment going before for the weakness and unprofitableness thereof"* (v. 18).

Such are the facts of history, but I am not about to expand upon them. I am coming to our own personal histories, to the experience of every child of God. In each and every one of us, it must be fulfilled that all that is of the flesh in us, when we see it as nothing but grass, must be withered, and the loveliness of it must be destroyed.

The Spirit of God, like the wind, must pass over the field of our souls and cause our beauty to be as a fading flower. He must so convince us of sin and so reveal ourselves to ourselves that we will see that the flesh profits nothing. Our fallen nature is corruption itself, and *"they that are in the flesh cannot please God"* (Romans 8:8). The sentence of death upon our former legal and carnal life must be brought home to us, so that the incorruptible seed of the Word of God, implanted by the Holy Spirit, may be in us and abide in us forever.

Implanting work always follows where withering work has been performed.

CAUSING THE UNGODLINESS OF THE FLESH TO FADE

The work of the Holy Spirit upon the soul of man in withering up that which is of the flesh is very unexpected. You will observe in our Scripture that even the speaker himself, though doubtless one taught of God, said, *"What shall I cry?"* (Isaiah 40:6). Even he did not know that there must first be an experience of preliminary visitation for the comforting of God's people.

Many preachers of God's Gospel have forgotten that *"Wherefore the law was our schoolmaster to bring us unto Christ, that we might be justified by faith"* (Galatians 3:24). They have sown on the unbroken, fruitless ground and have forgotten that the plow must break up the clods (Hosea 10:11). We have seen too much of trying to sew without the sharp needle of the convincing power of the Holy Spirit.

Preachers have labored to make Christ precious to those who think of themselves as rich and wealthy in goods. It has been labor in vain. It is our duty to preach Jesus Christ to even self-righteous sinners, but it is certain that they will never accept Jesus Christ while they hold themselves in high esteem. Only the sick will welcome the physician. It is the work of the Spirit of God to convince men of sin, and until they are convinced of sin, they will never be led to seek the righteousness that God gives by Jesus Christ.

I am persuaded that wherever there is a real work of grace in any soul, it begins with a pulling down. The Holy Spirit does not build on the old foundation. Wood, hay, and stubble will not do for Him to build upon. He will come as the fire and cause all of nature's proud idols to blaze. He will break our bows, cut our spears apart, and burn our chariots with His fire. When every sandy foundation is gone, and not until then, He will lay in our souls the great stone foundation, chosen by God, and precious.

Do you not see that it is divinely wise that you be stripped before you are clothed? Would you wear Christ's lustrous righteousness, which is whiter than any can make it, on the outside and conceal your own filthy rags inside? No, they must be put away. Not a single thread of your own must be left upon you. God may not cleanse you until He has made you see some of your defilement, for you would never value the precious *"blood of Jesus Christ his Son cleanseth us from all sin"* (1 John 1:7), if you had not first of all been made to mourn the fact that you are altogether an unclean thing.

The convincing work of the Spirit, wherever it comes, is unexpected. Even to the child of God in whom this process still has to go on, it is often startling. We begin to rebuild that which the Spirit of God has destroyed. Having begun in the Spirit, we act as if we will be made perfect in the flesh, and then when our mistaken building-up has to be leveled with the earth, we are almost as astonished as we were when the scales first fell from our eyes. Newton was in this sort of condition when he wrote,

> I asked the Lord that I might grow
> > In faith and love and every grace,
> Might more of his salvation know,
> > And seek more earnestly his face.
>
> 'Twas he who taught me thus to pray,
> > And he, I trust, has answered prayer;
> But it has been in such a way
> > As almost drove me to despair.
>
> I hoped that in some favored hour,
> > At once he'd answer my request,
> And by his love's constraining power.
> > Subdue my sins, and give me rest.

Instead of this, he made me feel
The hidden evils of my heart;
And let the angry powers of hell
Assault my soul in every part.

Marvel not, for the Lord is accustomed to answering His people. The voice that says, *"Comfort ye, comfort ye my people"* (Isaiah 40:1), achieves its purpose by first making them hear the cry, *"All flesh is grass, and all the goodliness thereof is as the flower of the field"* (Isaiah 40:6). If we consider well the ways of God, we should not be astonished that He begins with His people by revealing the terrible things before righteousness.

Observe the method of creation. I will not venture upon any dogmatic theory of geology, but there seems to be every probability that this world has been readied and destroyed many times before the last arranging of it for the habitation of men. *"In the beginning God created the heaven and the earth"* (Genesis 1:1). Then came a long interval, and at length, at the appointed time, during seven days, the Lord prepared the earth for the human race.

Consider the state of matters when the Great Architect began His work. What was there in the beginning? Originally, nothing. When He commanded the ordering of the earth, how did it happen? *"The earth was without form, and void; and darkness was upon the face of the deep"* (Genesis 1:2). There was no trace of another's plan to interfere with the Great Architect.

> *With whom took he counsel, and who instructed him, and taught him in the path of judgment, and taught him knowledge, and showed to him the way of understanding?* (Isaiah 40:14)

The Almighty received no contribution of columns or pillars toward the temple that He intended to build. The earth was, as the Hebrew puts it, *tohu* and *bohu*, disorder and confusion, or chaos.

So it is in the new creation as well. When the Lord creates us anew, He borrows nothing from the old man, but He makes all things new. He does not repair and add a new wing to the old house of our depraved nature, but He builds a new temple for His own praise. We are spiritually without form and empty. Darkness is upon the faces of our hearts, and His Word comes to us saying, *"Let there be light"* (Genesis 1:3), and there is light preceding long life and every precious thing.

Take another instance from the ways of God. When man has fallen, when does the Lord bring him to the Gospel? The first whisper of the Gospel was,

I will put enmity between thee and the woman, and between thy seed and her seed; it shall bruise thy head, and thou shalt bruise his heel. (Genesis 3:15)

That whisper came to man as he was shivering in the presence of his Maker, having nothing more to say by way of excuse, but standing guilty before the Lord. When did the Lord God clothe our parents? It was not until He first had asked the question, *"Who told thee that thou wast naked?"* (Genesis 3:11). Not until the fig leaves had utterly failed did the Lord bring in the covering skin of the sacrifice and wrap them in it.

If you will pursue the meditation upon the acts of God with men, you will constantly see the same thing. God has given us a wonderful type of salvation in Noah's ark, but Noah was saved in that ark in connection with death. He was, as it were, enclosed alive in a tomb, and all the world outside was left to destruction. All other hope for Noah was gone, but then the ark rose upon the waters.

Remember the redemption of the children of Israel from Egypt. It occurred when they were in the saddest situation, and their cries went up to heaven because of their bondage. No arm was bringing salvation until with a high hand and an outstretched arm, the Lord brought forth His people. Before salvation, there comes the humbling of the creature, the overthrow of human hope.

As in the backwoods of America before the cultivation of land, the planting of cities, the arts of civilization, and the transactions of commerce, the woodsman's ax must cut and sever the stately trees. Centuries must fall. The roots must be burned. The old reign of nature must be disturbed because the old must go before the new can come. Even the Lord takes away the first so that He may establish the second.

The first heaven and the first earth must pass away, or there cannot be a new heaven and a new earth. Now, as it has been outwardly, we ought to expect that it would be the same within us. When withering and fading occur in our souls, we should only say, *"It is the Lord: let him do what seemeth him good"* (1 Samuel 3:18).

Our Scripture shows that this withering process happens universally over the hearts of all those upon whom the Spirit works. The withering is a withering of what? Of part of the flesh and some portion of its tendencies? No. Observe, *"All flesh is grass, and all the goodliness thereof"* —the very choice and pick of it—*"is as the flower of the field"* (Isaiah 40:6). What happens to the grass? Does any of it live? *"The grass withereth"* (Isaiah 40:7). All of it. The flower, will that not live? So fair a thing, does it not have immortality? No, it fades. It utterly falls away.

So, wherever the Spirit of God breathes on the soul of man, there is a withering of everything that is of the flesh. It is seen that to be carnally minded is death. Of course, we all know and confess that where there is a work of grace, there must be a destruction of our delight in the pleasures of the flesh. When the Spirit of God breathes on us, that which was sweet becomes bitter, and that which was bright becomes dim. A man cannot love sin and yet possess the life of God. If he takes pleasure in the fleshly joys he once delighted in, he is still what he was. He minds the things of the flesh, and therefore, he is after the flesh, and he will die. The world and its lusts are as beautiful as the meadows in spring to the sinful, but to the renewed soul, they are a wilderness and uninhabited.

Of those very things we once delighted in, we say, *"Vanity of vanities; all is vanity"* (Ecclesiastes 1:2). We cry to be delivered from the poisonous joys of earth. We hate them and wonder how we could have ever enjoyed them. Do you know what this kind of withering means? Have you seen the lusts of the flesh and the pleasures fade away before your eyes? This must happen, or the Spirit of God has not visited your soul.

Whenever the Spirit of God comes, He destroys the goodliness and flower of the flesh. Our self-righteousness withers along with our sinfulness. Before the Spirit comes, we think of ourselves as the best. We say, "I have kept all the commandments since childhood," and we arrogantly ask, "What do I lack?" Have we not been moral? Have we not been religious? We confess that we may have committed faults, but we think they are very excusable. We venture in our wicked pride to imagine that we are not so bad, as the Word of God would lead us to think, after all. When the Spirit of God blows on the attractiveness of your flesh, its beauty will fade as a leaf, and you will have quite another idea of yourself. You will then find no language too severe in which to describe your past character. Searching deep into your motives and investigating that which moved you to your actions, you will see so much evil that you will cry with the tax collector, *"God be merciful to me a sinner"* (Luke 18:13).

While the Holy Spirit has withered the self-righteousness in us, He has not half completed His work. There is much more to be destroyed. Along with everything else, our boasted power of resolution must also go.

Most people formulate the idea that they can turn to God whenever they resolve to do so. "I am a man of such strength of mind," says one, "that if I made up my mind to be religious, I should be without difficulty."

"Oh," says another fleeting spirit, "I believe that one of these days I can correct the errors of the past and commence a new life."

These resolutions of the flesh are good flowers, but they must all fade. Even when the Spirit of God visits, we find that we do not act as we should. We discover that our wills are turned off to all that is good, and we naturally refuse to come to Christ so that we may have life. Resolutions are poor and frail when they are seen in the light of God's Spirit.

Still, a man will say, "I believe I have within myself an enlightened conscience and an intelligence that will guide me accurately. The light of nature I will use, and I do not doubt that I will find my way back again if I wander."

Man, your wisdom that is the very flower of your nature—what is it but folly? Yet, you do not see this. Unconverted and unrenewed, you are in God's sight no wiser than the colt of a wild ass. I wish you were humbled in your own esteem as a little child at Jesus' feet and made to cry, "Teach me."

When the withering wind of the Spirit moves over the carnal mind, it reveals the death of the flesh in all respects, especially in the matter of power towards that which is good. We then learn that Word of our Lord, "Without me ye can do nothing" (John 15:5). When I was seeking the Lord, I not only believed that I could not pray without divine help, but I felt in my very soul that I could not. I could not feel as accutely, or even mourn or groan as I would have. I longed to long more after Christ, but I could not even feel that I needed Him as I ought to have felt it.

This heart was then as hard, as adamant, and as dead as those that rot in their graves. Oh, what I would, at times, have given for a tear. I wanted to repent, but I could not. I longed to believe, but I could not. I felt bound, hampered, and paralyzed.

This is a humbling revelation of God's Holy Spirit but a needful one. The faith of the flesh is not the faith of God's elect. The faith that justifies the soul is the gift of God and not of ourselves. The repentance that is the work of the flesh will need to be repented of. The flower of the flesh must wither. Only the seed of the Spirit will produce fruit unto perfection. The heirs of heaven are *"born, not of blood, nor of the will of the flesh, nor of man, but of God"* (John 1:13). If the work in us is not the Spirit's working, but our own, it will droop and die when we require its protection most. Its end will be as the grass that is here today and tomorrow is gone.

Besides the universality of this withering work within us, notice also the completeness of it. The grass, what does it do? Droop? No, it withers. The flower of the field, what does it do? Does it hang its head a little? No, according to Isaiah it fades, and according to Peter it falls away. There is no reviving it with showers, for it has come to its end. The awakened are led to see that in their flesh dwells no good thing.

What dying and withering work some of God's servants have had in their souls! Look at John Bunyan as he described himself in his *Grace Abounding to the Chief of Sinners.* How many months and even years was the Spirit engaged in writing death upon all that was the old Bunyan in order that he might become by grace a new man, fitted to track the pilgrims along their heavenly ways!

We have not all endured the ordeal so long, but in every child of God, there must be a death to sin, to the law, and to self, which must be fully accomplished before he is perfected in Christ and taken to heaven. Corruption cannot inherit incorruption. It is through the Spirit that we mortify the deeds of the body and therefore live.

Can the fleshly mind not be improved? By no means, *"Because the carnal mind is enmity against God: for it is not subject to the law of God, neither indeed can be"* (Romans 8:7).

Can you not improve the old nature? No, *"Ye must be born again"* (John 3:7). Can it not be taught heavenly things? No, *"But the natural man receiveth not the things of the Spirit of God: for they are foolishness unto him: neither can he know them, because they are spiritually discerned"* (1 Corinthians 2:14).

There is nothing to be done with the old nature but to put it in the grave. It must be dead and buried. When this is so, the incorruptible seed that lives and abides forever will then develop gloriously. The fruit of the new birth will come to maturity, and grace will be exalted in glory. The old nature never does improve. It is as earthly, sensual, and devilish in the saint who is eighty years old as it was when first he came to Christ.

It is unimproved and unimprovable towards God. It is enmity itself. Every imagination of the thoughts of the heart is continuously evil. In the old nature, *"The flesh lusteth against the Spirit, and the Spirit against the flesh: and these are contrary the one to the other"* (Galatians 5:17). There cannot be peace between them.

Withering work in the soul is very painful. As you read these verses, don't they strike you as having a funereal tone? *"All flesh is grass, and all the goodliness thereof is as the flower of the field: The grass withereth, the flower fadeth"* (Isaiah 40:6–7). This is mournful work, but it must be done. I think that those who experience a great deal of it when they first come to Christ have much reason to be thankful. Their course in life will, in all probability, be much brighter and happier.

I have noticed that persons who are converted very easily and who come to Christ with relatively little knowledge of their own depravity have to learn it afterwards. They seem to remain babes in Christ for a long time, and they are perplexed with matters that would not have troubled them if they had experienced a deeper work at first. No, if grace has begun to build in your soul and any of the old walls of self-trust have been left standing, they will have to come down sooner or later.

You may congratulate yourself upon their remaining, but it is a false congratulation. Your glorying is not good. I am sure that Christ will never put a new patch on an old garment or new wine in old bottles. He knows it would be worse in the long run. All that is of nature's spinning must be unraveled. The natural building must come down—planks and plaster, roof and foundation—and we must have a house that is not made with the hands.

It was a great mercy for the city of London that the great fire cleared away all of the old buildings that were the resting place of the plague. A far healthier city was then built. Thus, it is a great mercy for a man when God sweeps away all of his own righteousness and strength, when He makes him feel that he is nothing and can be nothing, and when He drives him to confess that Christ must be all in all. Then, his only strength lies in the eternal might of the ever-blessed Spirit.

Although this is painful, it is inevitable. I have already shown you how necessary it is that all of the old should be taken away. However, let me further remark that it is inevitable that the old should go because it is in itself corruptible. Why does the grass wither? Because it is a withering thing. It must die. How could it spring out of the earth and be immortal? It is not a flower that never fades. It does not bloom in Paradise. It grows in soil on which the curse has fallen. Every supposed good thing that grows out of yourself is mortal, just like you, and it must die.

The seeds of corruption are in all the fruits of manhood's tree. Even if they are as fair to look upon as Eden's clusters, they must decay.

Moreover, it would never be acceptable to have something of the flesh in our salvation and something of the Spirit. If it were so, there would be a division of the honor—up to now the praises of God, beyond this will be my own praises. If I were to win heaven partly through what I had done and partly through what Christ had done, and if the energy that sanctified me was in a measure my own and in a measure divine, the reward should be divided. Thus, the songs of heaven, while they would be partly to the Almighty, they must also be partly to the creature. But, this will not be.

Down, proud flesh. Down, I say. Though you clean and purge yourself as you do, you are corrupt to the core. Though you labor unto weariness, you build wood that will be burned and stubble that will be turned to ashes. Give up your own self-confidence, and let the work and the merit be where the honor will be, namely, with God alone. It is inevitable, then, that there should be all this withering.

THE IMPLANTATION

According to Peter, although the flesh withers and the flower falls away, in the children of God, there is an unwithering something of another kind that does not wither. *"Being born again, not of corruptible seed, but of incorruptible, by the word of God, which liveth and abideth for ever"* (1 Peter 1:23). *"The word of the Lord endureth for ever. And this is the word which by the gospel is preached unto you"* (v. 25).

The Gospel is of use to us because it is not of human origin. If it were of the flesh, all it could do for us would not land us beyond the flesh. However, the Gospel of Jesus Christ is super-human, divine, and spiritual. In its conception, it was of God. Its great gift, even the Savior, is a divine gift, and all of its teachings are full of Deity.

If you believe a gospel that you have thought out for yourself or a philosophical gospel that comes from the brain of man, it is of the flesh. It will wither, and you will die and be lost through trusting in it. The only word that can bless you and that can be a seed in your soul must be the living and in-corruptible Word of the eternal Spirit.

Now, this is the incorruptible Word:

The Word was made flesh, and dwelt among us. (John 1:14)

God was in Christ, reconciling the world unto himself, not imputing their tres-passes unto them. (2 Corinthians 5:19)

Whosoever believeth that Jesus is the Christ is born of God. (1 John 5:1)

He that believeth on him is not con-demned: but he that believeth not is condemned already, because he hath not believed in the name of the only be-gotten Son of God. (John 3:18)

*God hath given to us eternal life, and
this life is in his Son.* (1 John 5:11)

Now, this is the seed, but before it can
grow in your soul, it must be planted there by
the Holy Spirit. Will you receive it? Then the
Holy Spirit implants it in your soul. Leap up
to it and say, "I believe it, and I grasp it. I fix
my hope on the incarnate God. The substitu-
tionary sacrifice and the complete atonement
of Christ is all my confidence. I am reconciled
to God by the blood of Jesus." Then, you possess the living seed within your soul.

What is the result of it? According to the
text, a new life comes into us as the result of
the indwelling of the living Word and our being born again by it. It is a new life. It is not
the old nature putting out its better parts and
not the old Adam refining, purifying itself,
and rising to something better. No, the flesh
withers, and its flower fades. It is an entirely
new life. You are just as much new creatures
at your regeneration as if you had never ex-
isted and had been created for the first time.
*"Therefore if any man be in Christ, he is a new
creature: old things are passed away; behold,
all things are become new"* (2 Corinthians
5:17).

The child of God is beyond and above
other men. Other men do not possess the life
that he has received. They have a body and a

soul, but he is spirit, soul, and body. A fresh principle, a spark of the divine life, has dropped into his soul. He is no longer a natural or carnal man, but he has become a spiritual man. He is understanding spiritual things and possessing a life far superior to anything that belongs to the rest of mankind. May God, who has withered that which is of the flesh in your souls, speedily grant you the new birth through the Word.

Now, wherever this new life comes through the Word, it is incorruptible. It lives and abides forever. To get the good seed out of a true believer's heart and to destroy the new nature in him is a thing that is attempted by earth and hell, but it is never achieved. Pluck the sun out of the sky, and even then, you will not be able to pluck grace out of a born-again heart. As 1 Peter 1:23 says, it *"liveth and abideth for ever."* It can neither corrupt itself nor be corrupted.

We know that whosoever is born of God sinneth not. (1 John 5:18)

I give unto them eternal life; and they shall never perish, neither shall any man pluck them out of my hand.
(John 10:28)

But whosoever drinketh of the water that I shall give him shall never thirst;

but the water that I shall give him shall
be in him a well of water springing up
into everlasting life.　　　(John 4:14)

You have a natural life that will die; it is
of the flesh. You have a spiritual life, and of
that it is written, *"And whosoever liveth and*
believeth in me shall never die. Believest thou
this?" (John 11:26). You now have within you
the noblest and truest immortality. You must
live as God lives—in peace, joy, and happiness.

Remember, if you do not have this, you
"shall not see life" (John 3:36). What then?
Will you be annihilated? No, but the wrath of
the Lord will be upon you (John 3:36). You
will exist, but you will not live. You will know
nothing of life, for life is the gift of God in
Christ Jesus. But, an everlasting death that
is full of torment and anguish will be on the
one who does not believe.

If you do not believe, you will be *"cast into*
the lake of fire. This is the second death" (Rev.
20:14). You will be one of those whose *"worm*
dieth not, [and whose] *fire is not quenched"*
(Mark 9:44). May God, the ever-blessed Spirit,
visit you. If He is now striving with you, do
not quench His divine flame.

Do not toy with any holy thought you
have. If you must confess that you are not
born again, be humbled by it. Go and seek

mercy from the Lord. Plead for Him to deal graciously with you and save you. Many who have had nothing but moonlight have received it, and before long, they have had sunlight.

Above all, remember what the quickening seed is, and reverence it when you hear it preached: *"This is the word which by the gospel is preached unto you"* (1 Peter 1:25). Respect it and receive it. Remember that the quickening seed is all wrapped up in this sentence, *"Believe on the Lord Jesus Christ, and thou shalt be saved"* (Acts 16:31). *"He that believeth and is baptized shall be saved; but he that believeth not shall be damned"* (Mark 16:16). The Lord bless you, for Jesus' sake. Amen.

FIVE

THE COVENANT PROMISE OF THE SPIRIT

And I will put my spirit within you, and cause you to walk in my statutes, and ye shall keep my judgments, and do them.
—Ezekiel 36:27

The tongues of men and of angels might fail. To call this verse a golden sentence would be much too commonplace, and to liken it to a pearl of great price would be too poor a comparison. We cannot feel, much less speak, too much in praise of the great God who has put this clause into the covenant of His grace. In that covenant, every sentence is more precious than heaven and earth, and this line is not the least among His choice words of promise: *"I will put my spirit within you."*

A GRACIOUS WORD

I would begin by expressing that it is a gracious word, but it was spoken to a graceless people. It was spoken to a people who had followed their own ways and refused the way of God. They were a people who had already provoked something more than ordinary anger in the Judge of all the earth.

For, He Himself said in Ezekiel 36:18, *"I poured my fury upon them."* These people, even under chastisement, caused the holy name of God to be profaned among the heathen wherever they went. They had been highly favored, but they abused their privileges and behaved worse than those who never knew the Lord. They sinned flagrantly, willfully, wickedly, proudly, and presumptuously; by this, they greatly provoked the Lord.

Yet, He made such a grace-filled promise to them as this: *"I will put my spirit within you."* Surely, *"where sin abounded, grace did much more abound"* (Romans 5:20). Clearly, this is a word of grace, for the law says nothing of this kind. Turn to the law of Moses, and see if there is any word spoken there that concerns the putting of the Spirit within men to cause them to walk in God's statutes. The law proclaims the statutes, but the Gospel alone promises the Spirit by which the statutes will be obeyed.

The law commands and makes us know what God requires of us, but the Gospel goes further and inclines us to obey the will of the Lord. It also enables us to practically walk in His ways. Under the dominion of grace, *"God...worketh in you both to will and to do of his good pleasure"* (Philippians 2:13).

So great a blessing as this could never come to any man by merit. A man might act as if he deserves a reward of a certain kind in a measure suited to His commendable action. However, the Holy Spirit can never be the wage for human service. The idea verges on blasphemy.

Can any man deserve Christ dying for him? Who would dream of such a thing? Can any man deserve the Holy Spirit dwelling in him and working holiness in him? The greatness of the blessing lifts it high above the range of merit. If the Holy Spirit is bestowed, it must be by an act of divine grace—grace infinite in bounty, exceeding all that we could have imagined. "Sovereign grace o'er sin abounding" is here seen in clearest light.

"I will put my spirit within you" is a promise that drips with grace as the honeycomb drips with honey. Listen to the divine music that pours from this word of love. I hear the soft melody of grace, grace, grace, and nothing else but grace. Glory be to God, who gives to sinners the indwelling of His Spirit.

A DIVINE WORD

"I will put my spirit within you" is also a divine word. Who but the Lord could speak in this way? Can one man put the Spirit of God within another? Could all of the church combined breathe the Spirit of God into a single sinner's heart? To put any good thing into the deceitful heart of man is a great achievement, but to put the Spirit of God into the heart is truly only done by the finger of God.

"The Lord hath made bare His holy arm" (Isaiah 52:10), and displayed the fullness of His mighty power. To put the Spirit of God into our nature is a work peculiar to the Godhead. To do this within the nature of a free agent, such as man, is marvelous.

Who but the God of Israel can speak after this royal style and beyond all dispute declare, *"I will put my spirit within you"*? Men must always surround their resolutions with conditions and uncertainties, but since omnipotence is at the back of every promise of God, He speaks like a king in a style that is only fit for the eternal God. He purposes and promises, and just as surely He performs. The promise of our sacred verse is certain to be fulfilled. It is certain because it is divine.

Oh, sinner, if we poor creatures had the work of saving you, we would break down in the attempt; but behold, the Lord Himself comes on the scene, and the work is done. All the difficulties are removed by this one sentence: *"I will put my spirit within you."* We have worked with our spirits, have wept over you, and have begged you, but we still have failed. However, there comes One into the matter who cannot fail. With Him, nothing is impossible. He begins His work by saying, *"I will put my spirit within you."* The Word is of grace and of God. Regard it, then, as a pledge from the God of grace.

AN INDIVIDUAL AND PERSONAL WORD

To me, there is much charm in the further thought that this is an individual and personal word. The Lord means, *"I will put my spirit within you,"* as individuals, one by one. This must be so since the connection requires it.

We read in Ezekiel 36:26, *"A new heart also will I give you."* Now, a new heart can only be given to one person. Each man needs a heart of his own, and each man must have a new heart for himself. The verse continues, *"And a new spirit will I put within you."* Within each one, this must be done, *"And I will take away the stony heart out of your flesh, and I will give you an heart of flesh."*

These are all personal, individual operations of grace. God deals with men one by one in the solemn matters of eternity, sin, and salvation. We are born one by one, and we die one by one. Even so, we must be born again one by one, and each one must receive the Spirit of God for himself. Without this, a man has nothing. Man cannot be caused to walk in God's statutes except by the infusion of grace into him as an individual.

I think I see among my hearers a single man or woman who feels himself or herself to be all alone in the world and therefore hopeless. You can believe that God will do great things for a nation, but how should the solitary be thought of? You are an odd person, one that could not be written down in any list. You are a peculiar sinner with constitutional tendencies all your own. God says, *"I will put my spirit within you."* That means within *your* heart. Yes, even *yours.* You who have long been seeking salvation but who have not known the power of the Spirit, this is what you need.

You have been striving in the energy of the flesh, but you have not understood where your true strength lies. God says to you in Zechariah 4:6, *"Not by might, nor by power, but by my spirit, saith the LORD of hosts,"* and again, *"I will put my spirit within you"* (Ezekiel 36:27). Oh, that this word might be spoken by the Lord to that young man who is ready to despair or to that sorrowful woman who has been looking into herself for power to pray and to believe.

You are without strength or hope in and of yourself, but this meets your case in all points. *"I will put my spirit within you"* means within you as an individual. Ask the Lord for it. Lift up your heart in prayer to God, and ask Him to pour upon you the Spirit of grace and of supplication. Plead with the Lord, saying, "Let your good Spirit lead me, even me." Cry, "Pass me not, my gracious Father, but in me fulfill this wondrous word of yours, *'I will put my spirit within you'*" (Ezekiel 36:27).

A SEPARATING WORD

This is also a separating word. I do not know whether you will see this readily, but it must be so. This word separates a man from his peers. Men, by nature, are of another spirit than that of God, and they are under subjection to that evil spirit, the Prince of the power of the air. When the Lord comes to gather out His own, fetching them out from among the heathen, He effects the separation by fulfilling this word, *"I will put my spirit within you"* (Ezekiel 36:27). After this is done, the individual becomes a new man.

Those who have the Spirit are not of the world nor like the world. They soon have to come out from among the ungodly and be separate, for differences of nature create conflict. God's Spirit will not dwell with the evil spirit. You cannot have fellowship with Christ and with Belial, with the kingdom of heaven and with this world.

I wish that the people of God would again awaken to the truth that to gather a people from among men is the great purpose of the present dispensation. It is still true, as James said at the Jerusalem Council, *"Simeon hath declared how God at the first did visit the Gentiles, to take out of them a people for his name"* (Acts 15:14).

We are not to cling to the old wreck with the expectation that we will pump the water out of her and get her safely into port. No, the cry is very different. "Take to the lifeboat! Take to the lifeboat! You are to leave the wreck. Then, you are to carry away from the sinking mass that which God will save." You must be separate from the old wreck, so it will not suck you down to sure destruction.

Your only hope of doing good to the world is by being *"not of the world"* (John 17:16), just as Christ was not of the world. If you sink down to the world's level, it will not be good for it or for you. What happened in the days of Noah will be repeated. When the sons of God entered into alliance with the daughters of men, and there was a league between the two races, the Lord could not endure the evil mixture. He drew up the passageway of the lower deep and swept the earth with a destroying flood.

Surely, in that last day of destruction, when the world is overwhelmed with fire, it will be because the church of God will have degenerated and the distinctions between the righteous and the wicked will have been broken down. The Spirit of God, wherever He comes, does speedily make and reveal the difference between Israel and Egypt. And in proportion as His active energy is felt, there will be an ever-widening gulf between those who are led by the Spirit and those who are under the dominion of the flesh. This is a separating word. Has it separated you? Has the Holy Spirit called you apart and blessed you? Do you differ from your old companions? Do you have a life that they do not understand? If not, may God, in mercy, put into you that most heavenly deposit, *"I will put my spirit within you"* (Ezekiel 36:27).

A UNITING WORD

It is also a very uniting word. It separates from the world, but it joins to God. *"I will put my Spirit within you"* (Ezekiel 36:27). It is not merely *a* spirit or *the* spirit, but *His Spirit*. Now, when God's own Spirit comes to reside within our mortal bodies, we are near kindred to the Most High. As 1 Corinthians 6:19 asks, *"Know ye not that your body is the temple of the Holy Ghost?"* Does this not make a man outstanding? Have you never stood in awe of your own self? Have you thought enough about how this poor body is sanctified, dedicated, and elevated into a sacred condition by being set apart as a temple of the Holy Spirit?

Therefore, are we brought into the closest union with God that we can well conceive of? Therefore, is the Lord our light and our life while our spirits are subordinate to the divine Spirit? *"I will put my spirit within you"* (Ezekiel 36:27).

God Himself then dwells in you. The Spirit of Him who raised Christ from the dead is in you. You life is hidden with Christ in God and the Spirit seals you, anoints you, and abides in you. By the Spirit, we have access to the Father. By the Spirit, we perceive our adoption and learn to cry, "Abba, Father." By the Spirit, we are made partakers of the divine nature and have communion with the threefold, holy Lord.

A CONDESCENDING WORD

I cannot help adding that it is a very condescending word. *"I will put my spirit within you"* (Ezekiel 36:27). Is it really true that the

Spirit of God, who displays the power and energetic force of God, by whom God's Word is carried into effect, who moved upon the face of the waters and brought order and life from chaos and death, is the One who lowers Himself to reside in men? God in our nature is a very wonderful conception. God in the babe at Bethlehem, God in the carpenter of Nazareth, God in the Man of Sorrows, God in the Crucified, and God in Him who was buried in the tomb—this is all marvelous.

The incarnation is an infinite mystery of love, but we believe it. Yet, if it were possible to compare one great wonder with another, I would say that God's dwelling in His people and that repeated ten thousand times over is more marvelous. That the Holy Spirit should dwell in millions of redeemed men and women is a miracle not surpassed by that of our Lord's adoption of human nature.

Our Lord's body was perfectly pure, and the Godhead, while it dwelt in His holy manhood, did at least dwell with a perfect and sinless nature. However, the Holy Spirit bows Himself to dwell in sinful men. He dwells in men who, after their conversions, still find the flesh warring against the spirit and the spirit against the flesh. He dwells in men who are not perfect even though they strive to be so. These men have to mourn their shortcomings and even have to confess with shame a measure of unbelief. *"I will put my spirit within you"* (Ezekiel 36:27) means that the Holy Spirit is in our imperfect nature. Wonder of wonders! Yet, it is as surely a fact as it is a wonder.

Believers in the Lord Jesus Christ, you have the Spirit of God, for *"if any man have not the Spirit of Christ, he is none of his"* (Romans 8:9). You could not bear the suspicion that you are not His. Therefore, as surely as you are Christ's, you have His Spirit abiding in you.

The Savior has gone away on purpose so that the Comforter may be given to dwell in you, and He does dwell in you. Is it not so? If it be so, admire this condescending God, and worship and praise His name. Sweetly submit to His rule in all things. Grieve not the Spirit of God. Watch carefully so that nothing comes into you that may defile the temple of God. Let the faintest warning of the Holy Spirit be law to you. It was a holy mystery that the presence of the Lord was especially within the veil of the tabernacle and that the Lord God spoke by Urim and Thummim to His people. It is an equally sacred marvel that the Holy Spirit now dwells in our spirits, abides within our nature, and speaks to us whatsoever He hears of the Father.

By divine impressions that the opened ear can comprehend and the tender heart can receive, He speaks still. May God help us to know His still, small voice so as to listen to it with reverent humility and loving joy. Then we will know the meaning of the words, *"I will put my spirit within you"* (Ezekiel 36:27).

A SPIRITUAL WORD

It is also a very spiritual word. *"I will put my spirit within you"* (Ezekiel 36:27) has nothing to do with our wearing a peculiar garb; that would be a matter of little worth. It has nothing to do with affectations of speech; those might readily become a deceptive peculiarity. Our text has nothing to do with outward rites and ceremonies either, but it goes much further and deeper.

It is an instructive symbol when the Lord teaches us our deaths with Christ by burial in baptism. It is also to our great profit that He ordains bread and wine to be tokens of our communion in the body and blood of His dear Son. Still, these are only outward things, and if they are unattended by the Holy Spirit, they fail to achieve the purpose of their design.

There is something infinitely greater in this promise: *"I will put my spirit within you"* (Ezekiel 36:27). I cannot give you the whole force of the Hebrew words translated *"within you,"* unless I paraphrase them a little.

My paraphrase is, "I will put my Spirit in the midst of you." The sacred deposit is put deep down into our life's secret place. God does not put His Spirit upon the surface of the man, but He puts it into the center of his being. The promise means, "I will put my spirit in your bowels, in your hearts, in the very core of you." This is an intensely spiritual matter without mixing anything material and visible. It is spiritual, you see, because it is the Spirit that is given, and He is given internally within our spirits.

AN EFFECTUAL WORD

Observe again that this word is a very effectual one. *"I will put my spirit within you, and cause you to walk in my statutes, and ye shall keep my judgments, and do them"* (Ezekiel 36:27). The Spirit is operative. First, it is operative upon the inner life in that it causes you to love the law of the Lord. Then, it moves you openly to keep His statutes concerning Himself and His judgments between you and your fellowman. If a man is whipped into obedience, it is of little worth, but when obedience springs out of a life within, it is a priceless breastplate of jewels. If you have a lantern, you cannot make it shine by polishing the glass outside. You must put a candle within it, and this is what God does.

He puts the light of the Spirit within us, and then our light shines. He puts His Spirit so deep down in the heart that the whole nature feels it, and it works upward like a spring from the bottom of a well. Moreover, it is so deeply implanted that there is no removing it. If it were in the memory, you might forget it. If it were in the intellect, you might err in it, but *within you* it touches the whole man and has dominion over you without fear of failure.

When the very kernel of your nature is quickened into holiness, practical godliness is adequately secured. Blessed is he who knows through personal experience our Lord's words: *"The water that I shall give him shall be in him a well of water springing up into everlasting life"* (John 4:14).

QUICKENING

Let me show you how the good Spirit manifests the fact that He dwells in men. Quickening is one of the first effects of the Spirit of God being put within us. We are dead by nature to all heavenly and spiritual things, but when the Spirit of God comes, we begin to live. The man visited of the Spirit begins to feel. The terrors of God make him tremble, and the love of Christ makes him weep. He begins to fear, and he begins to hope: a great deal of the first and a very little of the second, it may be. He learns spiritually to sorrow. He is grieved that he has sinned and that he cannot cease from sinning. He begins to desire what once he despised, especially desiring to find the way of pardon and reconciliation with God.

I cannot make you feel. I cannot make you sorrow because of your sin, and I cannot make you desire eternal life. However, it is all done as soon as this word is fulfilled by the Lord: *"I will put my spirit within you"* (Ezekiel 36:27). The quickening Spirit brings life to those dead in trespasses and sins. This life of the Spirit shows itself by causing the man to pray.

The cry is the distinctive mark of the living child. He begins to cry in broken accents, *"God be merciful to me a sinner"* (Luke 18:13). At the same time that he pleads, he feels the soft relenting of repentance. He has a new mind towards sin, and he grieves that he should have grieved his God. With this comes faith, perhaps feeble and trembling, only a touch of the hem of the Savior's robe, but still, Jesus is his only hope and his sole trust. To Him he looks for pardon and salvation. He dares to believe that Christ can save even him. Life comes into the soul when trust in Jesus springs up in the heart.

Remember, just as the Holy Spirit gives quickening at first, He must also revive and strengthen it. Whenever you become dull and faint, cry for the Holy Spirit. Whenever you cannot feel as devoted as you wish to feel and you are unable to rise to any heights of communion with God, plead our Scripture in faith, and beg the Lord to do as He has said, *"I will put my spirit within you"* (Ezekiel 36:27). Go to God with this covenant clause, even if you have to confess, "Lord, I am like a log. I am a helpless lump of weakness. Unless you come and quicken me, I cannot live for You." Plead persistently the promise, *"I will put my spirit within you"* (Ezekiel 36:27).

All the life of the flesh will produce is corruption. All of the energy that comes from mere excitement will die down into the black ashes of disappointment. The Holy Spirit alone is the life of the regenerated heart.

Do you have the Spirit? If you do have Him within you, do you only have a small measure of His life? Do you wish for more? Then, go to where you went at first. There is only one river of the water of life; draw from its floods. You will be lively, bright, strong, and happy enough when the Holy Spirit is mighty within your soul.

ENLIGHTENING

When the Holy Spirit enters, after quickening, He gives enlightening. We cannot make men see the truth. They are so blind, but when the Lord puts His Spirit within them, their eyes are opened. At first, they may see rather hazily, but they do see. As the light increases and the eye is strengthened, they see more and more clearly. What a mercy it is to see Christ, to look to Him, and to be enlightened. By the Spirit, souls see things in their reality. They see the actual truth of them and perceive that they are facts. The Spirit of God illuminates every believer and enables believers to see even more marvelous things out of God's law. However, this never happens unless the Spirit opens the eyes. The apostle speaks of being brought *"out of darkness into his marvellous light"* (1 Peter 2:9).

It is a marvelous light that comes to the blind and dead. It is marvelous because it reveals truth with clearness. When you get into a puzzle over the Word of the Lord, do not give up in despair, but believingly cry, "Lord, put Your Spirit within me." Here lies the only true light of the soul.

CONVICTION

The Spirit also works conviction. Conviction is more persuasive than illumination. It is the setting of a truth before the eye of the soul so as to make it powerful upon the conscience. I have spoken to many who know what conviction means, yet I will explain it from my own experience.

From my reading, I knew what sin meant. Yet, I never knew sin in its heinousness and horror until I found myself bitten by it as by a fiery serpent. I felt its poison boiling in my veins. When the Holy Spirit made sin appear as sin to me, I was overwhelmed by the sight. I would rather have fled from myself to escape the intolerable vision. A naked sin that is stripped of all excuses and set in the light of truth is worse to see than to encounter the devil himself.

When I saw sin as an offense against a just and holy God, committed by such a proud and yet insignificant creature as myself, I was extremely alarmed. Did you ever see and feel and identify yourself as a sinner? "Oh, yes," you say, "we are sinners." Do you mean it? Do you know what it means? Many of you are no more sinners in your own estimation than you are Hottentots. The beggar who exhibits a fake sore does not know disease. If he did, he would have enough of it without pretenses.

To kneel down and say, "Lord, have mercy upon us miserable sinners," and then to get up and feel yourself a very decent sort of body, worthy of commendation, is to mock almighty God. It is by no means a common thing to get hold of a real sinner, one who is truly so in his own esteem. However, it is as pleasant as it is rare, for you can bring to the real sinner the real Savior, and He will welcome him. I do not wonder that Hart said, "A sinner is a sacred thing. The Holy Spirit hath made him so."

The point of contact between a sinner and Christ is sin. The Lord Jesus gave Himself for our sins. He never gave Himself for our righteousnesses. He comes to heal the sick, and the point He looks to is our sickness. No one ever knows sin as his own personal ruin until the Holy Spirit shows it to him. Conviction regarding the Lord Jesus comes in the same way. We do not know Christ as our Savior until the Holy Spirit is put within us. Our Lord says, *"He shall receive of mine, and shall show it unto you"* (John 16:14). You never see the things of the Lord Jesus until the Holy Spirit shows them to you.

To know Jesus Christ as your Savior, as one who died for you in particular, is a knowledge that only the Holy Spirit imparts. Comprehending present salvation personally as your own comes by your being convinced of it by the Spirit. Oh, to be convinced of righteousness and acceptance in the Beloved. This conviction comes only from Him who has called you, even from Him of whom the Lord says, *"I will put my Spirit within you"* (Ezekiel 36:27).

THE COVENANT PROMISE OF THE SPIRIT

PURIFICATION

Furthermore, the Holy Spirit comes into us for purification. *"I will put my spirit within you, and cause you to walk in my statutes, and ye shall keep my judgments, and do them"* (Ezekiel 36:27). When the Spirit comes, He infuses a new life, and that new life is a fountain of holiness. The new nature cannot sin because it is born of God, and it is a living and incorruptible seed (1 Peter 1:23). (This life produces good fruit, and good fruit only.) The Holy Spirit is the life of holiness.

At the same time, the coming of the Holy Spirit into the soul gives a mortal stab to the power of sin. The old man is not absolutely dead, but it is crucified with Christ. It is under sentence, and before the eye of the law, it is dead. As a man nailed to a cross may linger long but cannot live, so the power of evil dies hard, but it must die. Sin is an executed criminal. Those nails that fasten it to the cross will hold it until no breath remains in it. God the Holy Spirit gives the power of sin its death wound. The old nature struggles in its dying agonies, but it is doomed, and it must die.

You will never overcome sin by your own power nor by any energy other than that of the Holy Spirit. Resolves may bind it, as Samson was bound with cords, but sin will snap the cords in half. The Holy Spirit lays the ax at the root of sin, and it must fall. The Holy Spirit within a man is *"the spirit of judgment, and...the spirit of burning"* (Isaiah 4:4). Do you know Him in that character?

As the Spirit of judgment, the Holy Spirit pronounces sentence on sin, and it goes out with the brand of Cain upon it. He does more. He delivers sin over to burning. He executes the death penalty on that which He has judged. How many of our sins have we had to burn alive! It has cost us no small pain to do it. Sin must be taken out of us by fire if no gentler means will serve, and the Spirit of God is a consuming fire. Truly, *"our God is a consuming fire"* (Hebrews 12:29).

They paraphrase it, "God out of Christ is a consuming fire," but that is not Scripture. It is, *"our God,"* our covenant God, who is a consuming fire to refine us from sin. Has the Lord not said, *"I will... purely purge away thy dross, and take away all thy* [sin]*"* (Isaiah 1:25). This is what the Spirit does, and it is by no means easy work for the flesh, which would spare many a flattering sin if it could.

The Holy Spirit whets the soul with purity until He saturates it. Oh, to have a heart saturated with holy influences until it is as Gideon's fleece, which held so much dew that Gideon could wring out a bowl full from it! Oh, if only our whole natures were filled with the Spirit, and we were sanctified wholly—body, soul, and spirit. Sanctification is the result of the Holy Spirit being instilled within us.

PRESERVATION

The Holy Spirit also acts in the heart as the Spirit of preservation. Where He dwells, men do not go back into ruin. He works in them a watchfulness against temptation day by day. He helps them to wrestle against sin. A believer would rather die ten thousand deaths than sin. He works in a believer's union to Christ, which is the source and guarantee of acceptable fruitfulness. He creates in the saints those holy things that glorify God and bless the sons of men.

All true fruit is the fruit of the Spirit. Every true prayer must be *"praying in the Holy Ghost"* (Jude 1:20). He helps our infirmities in prayer. Even the hearing of the Word of the Lord is of the Spirit, for John said, *"I was in the Spirit on the Lord's day, and heard behind me a great voice"* (Revelation 1:10). Everything that comes of the man or is kept alive in the man is first infused and then sustained and perfected of the Spirit. *"It is the spirit that quickeneth; the flesh profiteth nothing"* (John 6:63).

We never go an inch towards heaven in any other power than that of the Holy Spirit.

We do not even stand fast and remain steadfast except as we are upheld by the Holy Spirit. The vineyard that the Lord has planted, He also preserves. As it is written, *"I the LORD do keep it; I will water it every moment: lest any hurt it, I will keep it night and day"* (Isaiah 27:3). Did I hear that young man say, "I should like to become a Christian, but I fear I should not hold out? How am I to be preserved?" A very proper inquiry for *"He that endureth to the end shall be saved"* (Matthew 10:22).

Temporary Christians are no Christians. Only the believer who continues to believe will enter heaven. How, then, can we hold on in such a world as this? Here is the answer. *"I will put my spirit within you"* (Ezekiel 36:27). When a city has been captured in war, those who formerly possessed it seek to win it back again, but the king who captured it sends an army to live within the walls. He said to the captain, "Take care of this city that I have conquered, and do not let the enemy take it again."

So, the Holy Spirit is the army of God within our redeemed humanity, and He will keep us to the end. *"The peace of God, which passeth all understanding, shall keep your hearts and minds through Christ Jesus"* (Philippians 4:7). For preservation, then, we look to the Holy Spirit.

GUIDANCE

The Holy Spirit is also within us for guidance. The Holy Spirit is given to lead us into all truth. Truth is like a vast cave, and the Holy Spirit brings torches and shows us all the splendor of the roof. Since the passage seems intricate, He knows the way, and He leads us into the deep things of God. He opens up to us one truth after another by His light and His guidance. Thus, we are *"taught of the LORD"* (Isaiah 54:13).

He is also our practical guide to heaven, helping and directing us on the upward journey. I wish Christian people would more often inquire of the Holy Spirit as to guidance in their daily life. Do you not know that the Spirit of God dwells within you? You need not always be running to this friend and to that to get direction. Wait upon the Lord in silence. Sit still in quiet before the revelation of God. Use the judgment God has given you, but when that does not suffice, resort to Him whom Mr. Bunyan calls "the Lord High Secretary," who lives within, who is infinitely wise, and who can guide you by making you to hear a voice behind you saying, *"This is the way, walk ye in it"* (Isaiah 30:21).

The Holy Spirit will guide you in life. He will guide you in death, and He will guide you to glory. He will guard you from modern error and from ancient error, too. He will guide you in a way that you know not. Through the darkness, He will lead you in a way you have not seen. These things will He do unto you and not forsake you.

Oh, this precious Scripture. I seem to have before me a great cabinet full of jewels, rich and rare. May the Holy Spirit Himself come and hand these out to you, and may you be adorned with them all the days of your life.

CONSOLATION

Finally, *"I will put my spirit within you"* (Ezekiel 36:27) is by way of consolation, for His choice name is "The Comforter." Our God would not have His children unhappy, and therefore, He Himself in the third person of the blessed Trinity has undertaken the office of Comforter.

Why does your face wear such mournful colors? God can comfort you. You that are under the burden of sin, it is true no man can help you into peace, but the Holy Spirit can.

Oh, God grant Your Holy Spirit to every seeker who has failed to find rest. Put Your Spirit within him, and he will rest in Jesus. And, you dear people of God, who are worried, remember that worry and the Holy Spirit are very contradictory one to another. *"I will put my spirit within you"* (Ezekiel 36:27) means that you will become gentle, peaceful, resigned, and acquiescent in the divine will. Then, you will have faith in God that all is well. David says, *"God my exceeding joy"* (Psalm 43:4), and such He is to us. "Yes, mine own God is He."

Can you say, "My God, my God"? Do you want anything more? Can you conceive of anything beyond your God? Omnipotent to work all forever! Infinite to give! Faithful to remember! He is all that is good. Light only, for *"in him is no darkness at all"* (1 John 1:5). I have all light, yes, all things, when I have my God. The Holy Spirit makes us comprehend this when He is put within us.

Holy Comforter, abide with us, for then we enjoy the light of heaven. Then are we always peaceful and even joyful, for we walk in unclouded light. In You our happiness sometimes rises into great waves of delight as if it leaped up to the glory.

The Lord wants to make this Scripture your own, *"I will put my Spirit within you"* (Ezekiel 36:27). Hallelujah!

SIX

HONEY IN THE MOUTH

*He shall glorify me: for he shall receive
of mine, and shall show it unto you.
All things that the Father hath are mine:
therefore said I, that he shall take of mine,
and shall show it unto you.*
—John 16:14–15

These precious verses reveal the Trinity, and there is no salvation apart from the Trinity. It must be the Father, the Son, and the Holy Spirit. *"All things that the Father hath are mine"* (v. 15) says Christ, and the Father has all things. They were always His, are still His, always will be His, and they cannot become ours until they change ownership, until Christ can say, *"All things that the Father hath are mine."*

It is by virtue of the representative character of Christ standing as the surety of the

Covenant that the *"all things"* of the Father are passed over to the Son and that they might be passed over to us. *"For it pleased the Father that in him should all fulness dwell"* (Colossians 1:19). *"And of his fulness have all we received"* (John 1:16). But yet, we are so dull that even though the conduit pipe is laid to the great fountain, we cannot get at it. We are lame. We cannot reach there. In comes the third Person of the divine Unity, the Holy Spirit, and He receives of the things of Christ and then delivers them over to us. So, we do actually receive through Jesus Christ, by the Spirit, what is in the Father.

Ralph Erskine, in his preface to a sermon on John 16:15, has a notable piece. He speaks of grace as honey for the cheering of the saints, for the sweetening of their mouths and hearts. He says that in the Father,

> The honey is in the flower, which is at such a distance from us that we could never extract it. [In the Son] the honey is in the comb, prepared for us in our Emmanuel, God-Man, Redeemer, the Word that was made flesh, saying, *"'All things that the Father hath are mine,'* and mine for your use and [behalf]"*: it is in the comb. But then, next, we have honey in the mouth; the Spirit taking all things, and making application thereof, by showing them unto us, and

making us to eat and drink with Christ, and share of these *"all things"*; yea, not only eat the honey, but the honeycomb with the honey; not only His benefits, but Himself.

It is a very beautiful division of the subject. Honey is in the flower in God, as is mystery—really there. There never will be any more honey than there is in the flower. There it is. But how will you and I get at it? We do not have the wisdom to extract the sweetness. We are the as the bees that are able to find it. It is bee-honey, but not man-honey.

Yet, you see in Christ it becomes the honey in the honeycomb, and He is sweet to our taste as honey dropping from the comb. Sometimes we are so faint that we cannot reach out a hand to grasp that honeycomb. There was a time when our palates were so depraved that we preferred bitter things and thought them sweet.

Now that the Holy Spirit has come, we have the honey in our mouths and the taste that can enjoy it. Yes, we have now so long enjoyed it that the honey of grace has entered into our constitution, and we have become sweet unto God. His sweetness has been conveyed to us by this strange method.

I scarcely need to remind you to keep the existence of the Trinity prominent in your life.

Remember, you cannot pray without the Trinity. If the full work of salvation requires a Trinity, so does that very breath by which we live. You cannot draw near to the Father except through the Son and by the Holy Spirit. There is a trinity in nature undoubtedly. Certainly the need of a Trinity in the realm of grace constantly turns up. When we get to heaven, we will understand, perhaps, more fully what is meant by the Trinity in unity. But, if that is a thing never to be understood, we will at least comprehend it more lovingly.

We will rejoice more completely as the three tones of our music rise up in perfect harmony unto Him who is One and Indivisible and yet is Three—the forever blessed Father, Son, and Holy Spirit—one God.

I cannot open up the following point to you, but He must do it. We must have the Scripture acted out upon ourselves. *"He shall glorify me...He shall take of mine, and shall show it unto you"* (John 16:14–15). May it be so just now.

WHAT THE HOLY SPIRIT DOES

"He shall take of mine, and shall show it unto you" (John 16:15). It is clear that the Holy Spirit deals with the things of Christ. Do not let us strain at anything new. The Holy Spirit could deal with anything in heaven

above or in the earth beneath: the story of the ages past, the story of the ages to come, the inward secrets of the earth, and the evolution of all things, if there be an evolution. He could do it all.

Like the Master, the Holy Spirit can handle any topic He chooses, but He confines Himself to the things of Christ and therein finds unutterable liberty and boundless freedom.

The Holy Spirit still exists and works and teaches in the church. However, we have a test by which to know whether what people claim to be revelation is revelation or not: *"He shall receive of mine"* (John 16:14). The Holy Spirit will never go farther than the Cross and the coming of the Lord. He will go no farther than that which concerns Christ. *"He shall receive of mine."* His one vocation is to deal with the things of Christ. If we do not remember this, we may be carried away by vagaries, as many have been.

When a minister has spent all Sunday morning whittling a Scripture down to the small end of nothing, what has he done? He is a minister who professes to have been called by the Spirit to the job of talking of the things of Christ. A whole morning was spent with precious souls who were dying while he spoke to them, handling a theme that was not in the least relevant to the needs of his hearers.

Oh, imitate the Holy Spirit. If you profess to have Him dwelling in you, be moved by Him. Let it be said of you in your measure, as of the Holy Spirit without measure, *"He shall receive of mine, and shall show it unto you"* (John 16:14).

But, next, what does the Holy Spirit do? Why, He deals with feeble men. Yes, He dwells with us poor creatures. I can understand the Holy Spirit taking the things of Christ and rejoicing in them, but the marvel is that He should glorify Christ by coming and showing these things to us. And yet, it is among us that Christ is to get His glory. Our eyes must see Him. An unseen Christ is not very glorious, and the unknown things of Christ, the untasted and unloved things of Christ seem to have lost their brilliance to a high degree.

The Holy Spirit, therefore, feeling that to show a sinner the salvation of Christ glorifies Him, spends His time—and has been spending these centuries—in taking of the things of Christ and showing them to us. It is a great condescension on His part to show them to us, but it is a miracle too.

If it were reported that suddenly stones had life, hills had eyes, and trees had ears, it would be a strange thing. However, for us who were dead and blind and deaf in an awful sense (for the spiritual is more emphatic than the natural), for us to be so far gone and for the Holy Spirit to be able to show the things of Christ to us is to His honor. But, He does do it. He comes from heaven to dwell with us. Let us honor and bless His name.

I never could make up my mind which to admire most as an act of condescension: the incarnation of Christ or the indwelling of the Holy Spirit. The incarnation of Christ is marvelous that He should dwell in human nature. But, observe, the Holy Spirit dwells in human nature in its sinfulness, not in perfect human nature, but in imperfect human nature. He continues to dwell, not in one body that was fashioned strangely for Himself and was pure and without taint, but He dwells in our bodies. *"Know ye not that ye are the temple*[s] *of the Holy Spirit"* (1 Corinthians 6:19), which were defiled by nature and in which a measure of defilement still remains, despite His indwelling? In addition, this He has done these multitudes of years, not in one instance nor in thousands of instances only, but in a number that no man can count.

He continues still to come into contact with sinful humanity. Not to the angels nor to the seraphim, not to the cherubim nor to the host who have washed their robes and made them white in the blood of the Lamb does He show the things of Christ, but He will show them to us.

He takes of the words of our Lord—those that Christ spoke personally and those that Christ spoke by His apostles. Let us never allow anybody to divide between the Word of the apostles and the Word of Christ. Our Savior has joined them together. *"Neither pray I for these alone, but for them also which shall believe on me through their word"* (John 17:20).

If any begin rejecting the apostolic Word, they will be outside the number for whom Christ prays. They shut themselves out by that very fact. I wish that they would solemnly recollect that the Word of the apostles *is* the Word of Christ. He tarried not long enough after He had risen from the dead to give us a further exposition of His mind and will, and He could not have given it before His death because it would have been unsuitable. *"I have yet many things to say unto you, but ye cannot bear them now"* (John 16:12).

After the descent of the Holy Spirit, the disciples were prepared to receive that which Christ spoke by His servants Paul, Peter, James, and John. Certain doctrines that we are sometimes taunted about as being not revealed by Christ but by His apostles were all revealed by Christ, every one of them. They can all be found in His teaching, but they are very much in parable form. It was after He had gone up into glory and had prepared a people by His Spirit to understand the truth more fully that He sent His apostles. He says, "Go forth, and open up to those whom I have chosen out of the world the meaning of all I said." The meaning is all there, just as all the New Testament is in the Old.

The words of the Lord Jesus and the words of His apostles are to be explained to us by the Holy Spirit. We will never get at the center of their meaning apart from His teaching. We will never get at their meaning at all if we begin disputing about the words, saying, "Now, I cannot accept the words." If you will not have the shell, you will never have the chick. It is impossible.

"The words are not inspired," some say. If we have no inspiration in the words, we have got an intangible inspiration that oozes away between our fingers and leaves nothing behind. We must go and say,

> Great Master, we thank You for the Book with all our hearts, and we thank You for putting the Book into words. But now, good Master, we will not quibble over the letter, as did the Jews and the rabbis and the scribes of old and so miss Your meaning. Open wide the door of the words that we may enter into the secret closet of the meaning, and teach us this, we pray You. You have the key. Lead us in, we pray.

Dear friends, whenever you want to understand a text of Scripture, try to read the original. Consult anybody who has studied what the original means, but remember that the quickest way into a text is praying in the Holy Spirit. Pray the chapter over. I do not hesitate to say that if a chapter is read upon one's knees, looking up at every word to Him that gave it, the meaning will come to you with infinitely more light than by any other method of studying it. *"He shall glorify me: for he shall receive of mine, and shall show it unto you"* (John 16:14).

He will redeliver the Master's message to you in the fullness of its meaning, but I do not think that is all that the text means. *"He shall receive of mine"* (John 16:14). In the next verse, the Lord goes on to say, *"All things that the Father hath are mine"* (John 16:15). I do think that it means, therefore, that the Holy Spirit will show us the things of Christ.

Christ speaks as if He did not have any things just then that were especially His own, for He had not died, nor had He risen. He was not pleading then as the great Intercessor in heaven. All of that was to come. But still, He says, "Even now, all things that the Father has are mine: all His attributes, all His glory, all His rest, all His happiness, all His blessedness. All that is mine, and the Holy Spirit will show that to you."

However, I might almost read my text in another light, for He has died, risen, gone on high—and, lo, He is coming again. His chariots are on the way. Now, there are certain things that the Father has and that Jesus Christ has that are truly the things of Christ, emphatically the things of Christ. My prayer is that all preachers of the Gospel might have this Scripture fulfilled in them: *"He shall take of mine"*—My things—*"and shall show* [them] *unto you."*

Suppose that we are going to preach the Word soon, and the Holy Spirit reveals to us our Master in His Godhead. Oh, how we would preach Him as divine. How surely He can bless our congregations! How certainly He must be able to subdue all things unto Himself, seeing that He is very God of very God!

It is equally sweet to see Christ as man. Oh, to have the Spirit's view of Christ's manhood! May I distinctly be able to recognize that He is bone of my bone and flesh of my flesh; that in His infinite tenderness He will pity me and deal with my poor people and with the troubled consciences that are around me; and that I have still to go to them and tell them of the One who is touched with the feeling of their infirmities, having been tempted in all points just as they still are! Oh, if we once, no, if every time before we preach, we could get a view of Christ in His divine and human natures and come down fresh from that vision to speak about Him, what glorious preaching it would be for our people!

It is a glorious thing to get a view of the offices of Christ by the Holy Spirit, but especially of His office as the Savior. I have often prayed to Him, "You must save my people. It is no business of mine. I never set up in that line or put over my door that I was a savior, but You have been apprenticed to this trade. You have learned it by experience, and You do claim it as Your own honor. You are exalted on high to be a Prince and the Savior. Do Your own work, my Lord."

I took this Scripture and used it during a service, and I know that God blessed it when I said to them, "May the Holy Spirit show you that Christ is the Savior. A physician does not expect you to make any apologies when you call upon him because you are ill, for he is a physician, and he wants you in order that he may prove his skill. Christ is the Savior, and you need not apologize for going to Him because He cannot be the Savior if there is not somebody to be saved."

The fact is, Christ cannot get hold of us anywhere except by our sin. The point of contact between the sick one and the physician is the disease. Our sin is the point of contact between us and Christ. Oh, that the

Spirit of God would take of Christ's divine offices, especially that of the Savior, and show them unto us!

Did the Holy Spirit ever show you these things of Christ, namely, His covenant engagements? When He struck hands with the Father, it was so that He would bring many sons unto glory. That of those whom the Father gave Him, He would lose none, but they should be saved. He is under bonds to His Father to bring His elect home. When the sheep have to pass again under the hand of Him who tells them, they will go under the rod one by one, each one having the blood-mark. He will never rest until the number in the heavenly fold tallies the number in the Book of Life.

So I believe, and it has been delightful for me to have been shown this when I have gone to preach. On a dull, dreary, wet, foggy morning, only a few were present. Yes, but they are picked people, whom God has ordained to be there, and there will be the right number there.

I preach, and there will be some saved. I do not go at it by chance but guided by the blessed Spirit of God. I preach with a living certainty, knowing that God has a people whom Christ is bound to bring home, and bring them home He will. While He will see the distress of His soul, His Father will take delight in every one of them. If you get a clear view of that, it will give you backbone and make you strong. *"He shall take of mine, and shall show it* [My covenant engagements] *unto you'* (John 16:15), and when you see them, you will be comforted."

But beloved, the Holy Spirit favors you by taking what is peculiarly Christ's—namely His love—and showing that to you. We have seen it, and we have seen it sometimes more vividly than others. If the full blaze of the Holy Spirit were to be concentrated upon the love of Christ and our eyesight enlarged to its maximum capacity, it would be such a vision that heaven could not exceed it.

We should sit with our Bibles before us in our studies and feel Christ.

> *I knew a man in Christ above fourteen years ago, (whether in the body, I cannot tell; or whether out of the body, I cannot tell: God knoweth;) such an one caught up to the third heaven.*
>
> (2 Corinthians 12:2)

Oh, to see the love of Christ in the light of the Holy Spirit! When it is so revealed to us, it is not merely the surface that we see but the love of Christ itself.

You know that you have never really seen anything yet, strictly speaking. You only see the appearance of the thing—the light re-flected by it. That is all you see, but the Holy Spirit shows us the naked truth and reveals the essence of the love of Christ. That essence shows love without beginning, without end, without change, without limit. That love is set upon His people simply from motives within Himself and from no outside motive. What must it be, what tongue can tell? Oh, it is a ravishing sight!

I think that if there could be one sight more wonderful than the love of Christ, it would be the blood of Christ.

Much we talk of Jesu's blood,
But how little's understood!

It is the climax of God. I do not know of anything more divine. It seems to me as if all the eternal purposes worked up to the blood of the cross and then worked from the blood of the cross towards the outstanding con-summation of all things.

Oh, to think that He should become man. God has made spirit, pure spirit, embodied spirit, and then materialism. Somehow, as if He would take all up into one, the Godhead links Himself with the material. He wears dust about Him even as we wear it. Taking it all up, He then goes in that fashion and re-deems His people from all the evil of their souls, their spirits, and their bodies. He pours out a life that, while it was human, was so in connection with the divine that we speak correctly of "the blood of God."

Turn to the twentieth chapter of Acts, and read how the apostle Paul put it: *"Feed the church of God, which he hath purchased with his own blood"* (Acts 20:28). I believe that Dr. Watts is not wrong when he says, "God that loved and died." It is an incorrect accuracy, a strictly absolute accuracy of incorrectness. So it must be whenever the finite talks of the Infinite. It was a wonderful sacrifice that could absolutely obliterate, annihilate, and extinguish sin and all the traces that could possibly remain of it. He has finished the transgression, made an end of sins, made reconciliation for iniquity, and brought in everlasting righteousness (Daniel 9:24).

You have seen this, have you not? But, you have to see more of it yet, and when we get to heaven, we will then know what that blood means. With what vigor we will sing, "Unto Him who loved us and washed us from our sins in His own blood."

Will anybody be there to say, "Is not that the religion of the shambles?" The pagans blasphemously call it this. They will find themselves where they will wish they had believed "the religion of the shambles." I think that it will burn like coals into the soul of any man who ever dared to talk like that. He did his own willful deeds in spite of the blood of God, and by these will he be cast away forever.

May the Holy Spirit show you Gethsemane, Gabbatha, and Golgotha. Then, may it please Him to give you a sight of what our Lord is now doing. Oh, how it would cheer you up at any time when you were depressed to see Him standing and pleading for you. Do you not think that if your wife were ill, your child were sick, there was scant food in the cupboard, and you were to go out the backdoor and see Him with the breastplate on, all the stones glittering, your name there, and Him pleading for you, you would not go in and say, "There, wife, it is all right. He is praying for us"? Oh, it would be a comfort if the Holy Spirit showed you a pleading Christ.

Then, realize that He is reigning as well as pleading. He is at the right hand of God the Father, who has put all things under His feet, and He waits until the last enemy will lie there. Now, you are not afraid, are you, of those who have been snubbing you and opposing you? Remember, He has said,

> *All power is given unto me in heaven and in earth. Go ye therefore, and teach all nations...and, lo, I am with you alway, even unto the end of the world.*
> (Matthew 28:18–20)

Next, and best of all, may the Holy Spirit give you a clear view of His coming. This is our most brilliant hope to say, "Lo, He is coming." The bolder the adversary grows, the less faith there is, and when zeal seems almost extinct—these are the tokens of His coming. The Lord always said so and that He would not come unless there was a falling away first. So, the darker the night grows and the fiercer the storm becomes, the better will we remember that He of the lake of Galilee came to them upon the waves in the night when the storm was wildest.

Oh, what will His enemies say when He comes? When they behold the nail-prints of the Glorified and the Man with the thorn-crown. When they see Him really come, they that have despised His Word and His ever-blessed blood, how they will flee before that face of injured love.

We, on the contrary, through His infinite mercy, will say, "This is what the Holy Spirit showed us, and now we behold it literally. We thank Him for the foresights that He gave us of the joyful vision."

There is one point that I want you to recollect: When the Holy Spirit takes of the things of Christ and shows them to us, He has a purpose in so doing.

It is with you, with regard to the Spirit showing you things, as it was with Jacob.

You know Jacob was lying down and went to sleep, and the Lord said to him, *"The land whereon thou liest, to thee will I give it"* (Genesis 28:13). Now, wherever you go, throughout the whole of Scripture, if you can find a place where you can lie down, that is yours. If you can sleep on a promise, that promise is yours.

"Lift up now thine eyes," said God to Abraham, *"and look from the place where thou art northward, and southward, and eastward, and westward: For all the land which thou seest, to thee will I give it"* (Genesis 13:14–15). The Lord increases our holy vision of delighted faith, for there is nothing you see that you cannot also enjoy. All that is in Christ is there for you.

THE HOLY SPIRIT COMES TO GLORIFY CHRIST

"He shall glorify me" (John 16:14). The Holy Spirit never comes to glorify us, or to glorify a denomination, or, I think, even to glorify a systematic arrangement of doctrines. He comes to glorify Christ. If we want to be in accord with Him, we must minister in a manner that will glorify Christ.

If it is not distinctly my aim to glorify Christ, I am not in accord with the aim of the Holy Spirit, and I cannot expect His help. We would not be pulling the same way. Therefore, I will have nothing of which I cannot say that it is said simply, sincerely, and only that I may glorify Christ.

How, then, does the Holy Spirit glorify Christ? It is very beautiful to think that He glorifies Christ by showing Christ's things. If you wanted to do honor to a man, you would perhaps take him a present to decorate his house. But here, if you want to glorify Christ, you must go and take the things out of Christ's house, "the things of Christ."

Whenever we are praising God, what do we do? We simply say what He is. "You are this, and You are that." There is no other praise. We cannot fetch anything from elsewhere and bring it to God, but the praises of God are simply the facts about Himself.

If you want to praise the Lord Jesus, tell people about Him. Take of the qualities of Christ, and show them to people. Thus, you will glorify Christ.

Alas, I know what you will do. You will weave words together, and you will form and fashion them in a marvelous manner until you have produced a charming piece of literature. When you have carefully done that, put it in the fire in the oven, and let it burn. Possibly, you may help to bake some bread with it. It is better for us to tell what Christ is than to invent ten thousand fine words of praise in reference to Him. *"He shall glorify me: for He shall receive of mine, and shall show it unto you"* (John 16:14).

Again, I think that the blessed Spirit glorifies Christ by showing us the things of Christ *as Christ's*. Oh, to be pardoned! Yes, it is a great thing, but to find that pardon in His wounds, that is a greater thing. Oh, to get peace! Yes, but to find that peace in the blood of His Cross. Have the blood-mark very visibly on all your mercies. They are all marked with the blood of the Cross, but sometimes we think so much of the sweetness of the bread or of the coolness of the waters that we forget from where and how they came to be. They lack their choicest flavor.

That it came from Christ is the best thing about the best thing that ever came from Christ. That He saves me is somehow better than my being saved. It is a blessed thing to go to heaven, but I do not know that it is not a better thing to be in Christ and so, as the result of it, to get into heaven.

It is He, Himself, and what comes from Him that becomes best of all because it comes from Himself. The Holy Spirit will glorify Christ by making us see that these things from Christ are indeed of Christ, completely from Christ, and still in connection with Christ, and we only enjoy them because *we* are in connection with Christ.

Then it is said in the text, *"He shall glorify me...He shall take of mine, and shall show it unto you"* (John 16:14–15). Yes, it does glorify Christ for the Holy Spirit to show Christ to us. Often I have wished that men of great minds might be converted. I have wished that we could have a few Miltons and like men to sing of the love of Christ; a few mighty men who teach literature and philosophy to devote their talent to the preaching of the Gospel.

Why is it not so? Well, it is because the Holy Spirit does not seem to think that that would be the way to glorify Christ supremely. He prefers, as a better way, to take us commonplace people and to show us the things of Christ. He does glorify Christ. Blessed be His name that ever my bleary eyes should look upon His infinite loveliness. That ever such a wretch as I, who can understand everything but what I ought to understand, should be made to comprehend the heights and depths and to know with all saints the love of Christ that passes knowledge (Ephesians 3:18–19).

You see that clever boy in school; well, it is not much for the master to have made a scholar of him. But, here is one who shines as a scholar, and his mother says that he was the greatest dolt in the family. All his school fellows say, "Why, he was our slowest child! He seemed to have no brains, but our master somehow got some brains into him and made him know something, which he appeared at one time incapable of knowing." Somehow, it seems to be as if our very folly, impotence, and spiritual death will go towards the increase of that great glorifying of Christ at which the Holy Spirit aims if the Holy Spirit shows to us the things of Christ.

Then, since it is for the honor of Christ for His things to be shown to men, He will show them to us so that we may go and show them to other people. This we cannot do except when He is with us to make the others see. But, He will be with us while we tell what He has taught us, and the Holy Spirit will really be showing to others while He is showing to us. A secondary influence will flow from this service, for we will be helped to use the right means to make others see the things of Christ.

THE COMFORTER

It is the Comforter that does this, and we will find our richest, surest comfort in this work of the Holy Spirit who will take of the things of Christ and show them unto us.

First, He does so because there is no comfort in the world like seeing Christ. He shows us the things of Christ. Oh, if you are poor and if the Holy Spirit shows you that Christ had no where to lay His head, what a sight for you! If you are sick and the Holy Spirit shows you what sufferings Christ endured, what comfort comes to you! If you are made to see the things of Christ, each thing according to the condition that you are in, how speedily you are delivered out of your sorrow!

If the Holy Spirit glorifies Christ, that is the cure for every kind of sorrow. He is the Comforter. Many years ago, after the terrible accident in the Surrey Gardens, I had to go away into the country and keep quite still. The very sight of the Bible made me cry. I could only stay alone in the garden, and I was heavy and sad. People had been killed in the accident, and there I was half-dead myself.

I remember how I got back my comfort, and I preached on the Sunday after I recovered. I had been walking around the garden, and I was standing under a tree. If the tree is there now, I would know it. There I remembered these words: *"Him hath God exalted with his right hand to be a Prince and a Saviour"* (Acts 5:31). "Oh," I thought to myself, "I am only a common soldier. If I die in a ditch, I do not care. The king is honored. He wins the victory."

I was like those French soldiers in the old times who loved the emperor. You know how, when they were dying, if the emperor rode by, the wounded man would raise himself up on his elbow and cry once more, *"Vive l'Empereur!"* The emperor was engraved on his heart. And so, I am sure, it is with every one of you, my comrades, in this holy war. If our Lord and King is exalted, then let other things go whichever way they like. If He is exalted, never mind what becomes of us.

We are a set of pygmies, and it is all right if He is exalted. God's truth is safe, and we must be perfectly willing to be forgotten, derided, slandered, or anything else that men please. The cause is safe, and the King is on the throne. Hallelujah! Blessed be His name!

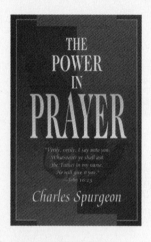

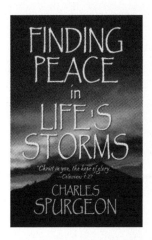

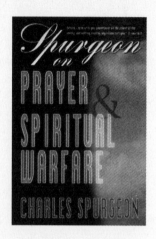